Collectanea to an Encounter

with Idealism

✳✳✳

Prologus: Intellectus quaerens
veritatem reorum

Leonard P. Wessell, jr.
Ph. D. (USA), Dr. phil. (Germany), Doctorado (Spain)

Berichte aus der Philosophie

Leonard Wessell

Collectanea **to an Encounter with Idealism**

Prologus: Intellectus quaerens veritatem reorum

Shaker Verlag
Düren 2022

Bibliographic information published by the Deutsche Nationalbibliothek
The Deutsche Nationalbibliothek lists this publication in the Deutsche
Nationalbibliografie; detailed bibliographic data are available in the Internet at
http://dnb.d-nb.de.

Printed in Germany.

ISBN 978-3-8440-8799-4
ISSN 0945-0947

Shaker Verlag GmbH • Am Langen Graben 15a • 52353 Düren
Phone: 0049/2421/99011-0 • Telefax: 0049/2421/99011-9
Internet: www.shaker.de • e-mail: info@shaker.de

IRENE
With Loving Memory and Gratitude

Si nada nos salva de la muerte,
Al menos que el amor nos salve de la vida.

Pedro Neruda

Table of Contents

Introduction

The first word of the title is *collectanea*, i.e., a collection, and with good reason. With the exception of Chapter 5, all other chapters represent a series of articles I published in the *Journal of Sino-Christian Studies* between the years 2009 and 2020. The titles are

1 "Free Reason / Free Will: An Exposition and Critique of Sam Harris' Argument Against Free Will", in Sino-Christian Studies, no. 30 (2007), 7-32.

2 "The Being of Truth Critical Reflections on Richard Rorty's Denial of Truth", in Sino-Christian Studies. no. 15 (2013), 59-98.

3 "Definitions of Infinity: An Attempt to Gain Conceptual Clarity with Mathematical and Theological Ramifications", in Sino-Christian Studies, no. 12 (2011), 67-103.

4 "The Ontological Argument: Reconstructed According to the Idealism of Josiah Royce", in Sino-Christian Studies, no. 8 (2009), 53-80.

To these articles I will attach an epilogue in which I will seek to draw a few themes together so as to present the prime assumptions of idealism as I see it. The articles, brought into a collectanea, have not been ordered according to the year of publication, rather according to thematic intension ordering the chapters in this book. It is this "intention" that I wish to make clear to my reader by explaining it in the introduction. The specific principle of ordering the narrative was not present in my mind before writing the articles. In no way were the articles written such that they might later be collected together as an extended discussion of a specific matter. Whereas there was no common principle motivating the articles, there was a common point of view, a common generative manner of thinking, that weaves its way through all the articles, some more clearly than others. What is this way? What directs my mode of thinking philosophically about different themes?

The answer is of course the philosophy designated as idealism. In my case, my philosophical origins are rooted in the "Absolute Idealism" of Anglo-American thinkers. How to define such an idealism, particularly its relevance as an organizing principle for this study? This is not easy matter as different commentators often disagree. However, while writing about the thought of Karl Jaspers, Wolfgang Stegmüller offers a short definition for idealism, one not without reference to the ensuing study. Stegmüller writes:

> Idealism [in opposition to realism] equates being (*Sein*) with the being of the mind [or the mental] (*Geist*), ascribes to the subject preference against

the objective, ascribes true reality [*Wirklichkeit*] to the being (*Sein*) of the idea[1].

The definition is anything but adequate, maybe even a bit obtuse for those not familiar with idealism; nevertheless, it does indicate the general nature of the articles to be reprinted in this book and will find a sort of summation in my epilogue. Although the themes of each article are proper unto themselves, i.e., each stands alone as a separate publication and needs no reference to others for comprehension, they all, nevertheless, reflect my idealistic stance, my way of philosophizing, or, in the terms of Stegmüller's definition, the articles are centered on the mental, the ideal, consciousness, and the subjective. In the final chapter, viz., addendum to the ontological argument, I will attempt to draw some unifying conclusions from the articles by explicating my understanding of the underlying principles to idealism, finally contrasting them with the principles of realism (particularly as defined by Nicolas Rescher). It is my hope that my presentation will elicit in my reader some understanding of and even some sympathy for idealism.

I have structured my presentation of the articles in order, hopefully, to enable my reader to accumulate slowly an insight into idealism, indeed, an insight that could be designated as an "encounter" with idealism as I wrestle intellectually with various problems that have motivated me to write and now to order them as collectanea. In no way, do I claim that any one article is a strict logical prerequisite of the next chapter. I only have sought to distill some common thread linking the articles in the order presented by the chapters. I will briefly indicate something about each article/chapter.

Chapter 1: Throughout my argument I have sought to think rationally. Yet, a determinist such as the preaching atheist, Sam Harris, holds that the human brain entirely "dictates to" human consciousness all and everything, every idea, every emotion, every thought, every argument, every want, every choice, every decision, all acts of willing, including all intellectual deliberation. The individual has no control over consciousness. If Harris is correct, my articles, products of my reason, are just illusions. But, I do not hold Harris' argument to be correct, on the contrary. If it is true, then Harris undercuts his own rationality, hence his argument is a mere dictation by forces beyond his consciousness, namely his brain dictated it. My point is to affirm Bernard Lonergan who maintains that we humans do possess a "pure desire to know", i.e., a cognitive motivation to seek to understand and affirm what is according to rational criteria. This is an important prerequisite for the arguments of any thinker, including myself. Also, this "pure desire to know" presupposes "pure reason" interacting with "pure willing", i.e., reason following its own canons which the will freely chooses to affirm. As an absolute prerequisite for my study, I do claim for myself a "pure willing to know", relative to which I possess a "pure", viz., "free" reason". It does not guarantee that I will find the truth, only that I *authentically* seek it. This, alas, cannot be said of Harris. Autonomous reasonable thinking grounds the possibility of encounters with what is.

Chapter 2: The theme is not the provocative question concerning just what truth is, rather pursues an attempt to determine how truth comes to be appropriated in human consciousness, that is, what the very being of truth (*esse veritatis*) is examined. It is argued that there is no truly grasped truth that is not eternal, i.e., its validity holds forever, a thesis which has ontological implications of a theological nature. The argument presented entails the first encounter with idealism.

Chapter 3: Infinity is a concept that enters into myriads of disciplines, form mathematics, science, engineering, simply counting or speculating about God or the absolute mind/consciousness of idealism. The method of deriving a concept of infinity, however, is two-fold. First and foremost, the concept of infinity is derived *extrapolatively*, i.e., 1, 2, 3, ... ∞. Such a concept has, mildly expressed, been the object of much contention, seemingly finding a solution in the thought of Cantor. Seemingly! There a second method of deriving infinity, namely an *exclusionary* method, i.e., excluding all finitude from infinity, leaving it as pure magnitude. This magnitude is examined in some of its mathematical and theological ramifications.

Chapter 4: In a somewhat light and ironic manner, Josiah Royce's ontological argument is examined, particularly for its critique of realism. Realism argues for and presupposes "independence" of beings from the mental *per se* as a constitutive mark of reality, a supposed mark that Royce criticizes heavily and in terms of which he offers his own counter argument, which entails his idealism. This is perhaps the most important "encounter" with idealism.

Epilogue: This chapter seeks to distill, formulate and defend the primary features of idealism, simultaneously criticizing the primary features of realism. The failures of "independence" typifying realist ontology are heavily criticized and the "dependency" of object and subject is revealed as the heart of idealism. Indeed, if my reader be primarily interested in the nature of idealism *per se* as opposed to my use of it in various chapters, then I recommend turning first to the epilogue. One might say, Royce's has so influenced me, that I have adopted his habit of saying what I really wanted to say in a supplement, viz. epilogue. The presentation of idealism does not depend upon the knowledge of what the chapters have to communicate. Idealism informs, quite certainly, the chapters.

Footnotes

1 Stegmüller, *Hauptströmungen der Gegenwartsphilosophie. Eine Kritische Einführung. Band I,* 7. Auflage, (Stuttgart: Alfred Kröner Verlag, 1989).

Chapter 1

Free Reason / Free Will:

Abstract

In the year 2012, *anno Domini*, Sam Harris, an evangelizing atheist, published a short, but quite challenging book with the title *Free Will*, a power that is, he argues, but an illusion. The conscious mind, its acts of minding and its contents are revealed to be fully determined by the brain. It follows from such complete determinism that the human mind lacks all autonomy and cannot, therefore, be responsible for its thoughts and deeds. Harris' argument against free will shall be submitted to a critical examination and then to a refutation in terms of my counter theory of free reason and free will. The task: I shall in the ensuing sections consider the fundamental contradiction in the argumentation of Harris, a self-contradiction Harris must bear, if intellectual honesty is to be observed. Certainly, a contradiction in theory constitutes a fragile basis for systematic consistency. Beyond that, I shall briefly take up a few derivative difficulties attendant to his think and offer a counter proposal concerning the relationship between free reason and free will.

Key Words: will, reason, freedom, necessity, reductionism

Introduction

In the year 2012, *Anno Domini*, Sam Harris, an evangelizing atheist, published a short, but quite challenging book with the title *FREE WILL*, a power that is, he argues, but an illusion[1]. The conscious mind, its acts of minding and its contents are revealed to be fully determined by the brain. For instance, because a neurophysical determinism completely controls the human mind, humans lack all autonomy and are, therefore, not responsible for their thoughts and deeds. Harris' argument will be submitted to a critical examination, indeed, to a refutation, along with my counter theory of *free* reason and *free* will[2]. In short, there is no reason without it being free and no freedom without reason.

Such a challenge to human autonomy is nothing new in the history of thought and is frequently seen as signifying, *nolens-volens,* a deterministic nihilism. This, of course, is not Harris' conclusion. Not at all! On the contrary, as is evident in subsequent books, Harris, proceeding from the basis of his denial, feels himself enabled, indeed, "freed" to preach the "good tidings" that liberate consciousness. Indeed, as I shall note below, Harris seems to affirm a modern form of gnostic release from the tyranny of each person's evanescent "I's"; a freedom entailing salvific dimensions (though he would probably disdain such vocabulary)[3]. Whatever, I enthusiastically greet the opening statement that commences Harris' argumentation, accepting it without reserve. Harris proclaims:

> The question of free will touches nearly everything we care about. Morality, law, politics, religion, public policy, intimate relationships, feelings of guilt and personal accomplishment—most of what is distinctly *human* about our lives seems to depend upon our viewing one another as autonomous persons, capable of free choice (*FW*, 1).

The reality or not of "*autonomous* persons" certainly embodies momentous concern. The enormity of the matter is simply stunning. Harris is to be sincerely thanked for bringing it up, and for presenting his views in a well written and easily readable booklet, never dull, always provocative, though a tale told at times a bit scant on reflective theory, however rich it may be in edifying exemplifications. And all this within a mere 83 pages (only 67 of which constitute the text)! Excellent preaching! Razor sharp reasoning, always within the framework of the 21st Century science triumphantly professed by Harris, leads him to conclude: "Free will *is* an illusion. Our wills are simply not of our making" (*FW*, 5). I presume that Harris would not object if I rephrased the last quotation by placing the words directly into his' singular mouth. In this case, referring to himself, Harris would then say: ‹‹*My* [supposed] free will *is* an illusion. *My* will is simply not of *my* own making››. And this assertion must be true for every single thinking human and imbued by everyone, once having become accepted, who would humbly confess the same thing. In short, my interpretation of Harris' thesis is that the ascription of "auton-omy" to the human will is an error, is definitively not the truth. Let us consider briefly what "autonomy" could mean. The "-*nom*-" in the term, as I interpret mat-ters, semantically indicates the "law" (or dynamic principle) that determines (or-ders, directs) the *how*, according to which the "auto-" (i.e., the "self or the "I") can and will consciously act, think, feel, want or choose. There is, if I grasp Harris' drift of thought, no structure indigenous to, no energy constitutive of, no causal power emerging from within the "self" that can constitute it as an independently dy-namic mental reality, whose mental operations are carried out by the conscious-ness' own "I". In no way is the operational self, i.e., the "I", volitionally self-pro-pelling! Indeed, such autonomy of the will, if things of nature truly were so, would mean that the "I" is able to function ***free*** from *all*-determinant factors external to the cognitive decisions of the intellect. Such *autonomy* has no ontological niche in Harris' view of deterministic nature as apparently conceived by 21st Century sci-ence. So, here Harris stands, he cannot do otherwise! It is, however, just such a thesis that I intend to reflect upon and critically evaluate, paradoxically using the very logic underlying Harris' argumentation so as to show that his "rational" use of 21st Century science is simply not possible, even contradictory in its application. Within that framework, it will become clear why Harris literally cannot find his mind. In other words, Harris' up-to-date science, ***if true***, sadly vitiates the very rationality used to ground said science. But, on the other hand, ***if reason is to lay claims to truth*** for propositions of science, then the all-determining science loses its universality, its reality thereby becoming more complicated than what monistic science can materialistically endure. The problem of free as will be seen reveals itself to be more complex than Harris has grasped. No free will, no reason! No free reason, no autonomous will. No autonomous will, no application of 21st Century science. A vicious circle arises. The carnivorous snake eats its mindless tail and dies of cognitive indigestion.

Before, however, undertaking my critical interpretation of Harris' argumentation, I first want to indicate why I have designated Harris as a preacher of "the good tidings". I am not trying to be facetious at all, rather factual. Harris is not a dull and abstract opponent of theism, free will and religion. The opening statement by Harris establishes what is of utmost importance for him relative to the problem-atic of free will. I too find such values of high importance. Such values point to the areas of human existence that well might be viewed as spirituality, previously un-der the domain of religion. There must be a very strong reason behind Harris' thinking if such sacred values are to be exposed to jeopardy. Yet I find that Harris' "formal" proof against free will, such as it is at all formal, lacks philosophical depth as well evidenced by miniscule space dedicated to it. The rest of his text is devoted to a plethora of implications and exemplifications following from the denial of free will.

Harris is a brilliant intellectual with specialization in neurology, whose main literary efforts have *not* been focused upon a dry logical argumentation, particularly of an ontological or metaphysical nature, against the existence of god or of free will. For instance, any real philosophical discussion of what is "existence" is conspicuously absent, let alone missing ruminations about such abstract notions such as "nature" and "reality" and "time". The terms just pop up, and that is it. Harris does not *even* offer a philosophy of science, relative to which modern physics is ordered and perhaps limited in scope. The assumption is simply that a deterministic modern 21st science, particularly the branch of neurology, is *the* one and only conceptual tool for any rational discussion of the mind. No deeper philosophy demanded. When it comes to denying divine existence or free will, Harris, although using the full weight of his considerable neurological and biological knowledge, theorizes in a most perfunctory manner against free will, yet quite effectively (until one probes the argument). Once his refutation is finished, Harris utilizes said conclusions to wander critically through many fields such a religion, morality, politics, and others mentioned in the above quotation. In his subsequent book, *The Moral Landscape*, Harris applies all his considerable acumen in order to show that science can determine human values. "Reality", though being only open to modern 21st Century science, is not valueless as many scientists have claimed. On the contrary, science can cast light upon the moral sciences. Science thereby replaces any traditional or biblical sources as *the* means for the cultural edification of the human race. Harris desperately wants to refute the myriad of scientists who deny that science can engender and project value judgments functioning as a morality that can govern human cooperation. In his *Waking Up* Harris treats such themes as spirituality, consciousness, the Self, meditation and even gurus and death. Particularly within the framework of consciousness (despite all efforts of science at Harris' disposal, consciousness itself distinctly remains a mystery to him), Sam Harris strikes me as having *de facto* formulated a *gnosticism* of effective salvation—a matter to be discussed at the finale of this study. It is because of the traits just listed that I find it fair to designate Harris as a preacher, be it an atheist one. However, much Harris is a preacher, he is of a certain rationalizing type. And that type implies what?

Preacher Harris in a distant, yet distinct manner reminds me of Bishop Fulton Sheen (1895-1979), certainly a preacher of significant success[3]. The similarity between the two is one of high intellectuality, the difference is one of the specifics of fundamental knowledge. Sheen was a very precocious student who delved into the realm of philosophy, metaphysics and the philosophy of science. These were his concerns before seriously taking up priestly duties—one central area of which can well be called "preaching". The edification Bishop Sheen sought to "preach" for the benefit of his audiences centered upon his rational explanation of why "life is worth living". Indeed, Bishop Sheen wrote a book with this title and pursued a popular tv show of the same title[4]. Sheen was admired by Catholics and Protestants and even some unbelievers. Sheen expanded the thesis of life as worthwhile subsequently in many books, just as Harris is now doing. However, before he commenced his serious "preaching", Bishop Sheen obtained a doctorate in philosophy (Thomism), reflected seriously upon his *The Philosophy of Science*, *Religion Without God* and even critiqued some of the best thinkers of this day in *God and Intelligence in Modern Philosophy*[5]. I confidentially conclude from the lives and works of both Sheen and Harris present us with a similar lifestyle of intellectuality and preaching. Intellectuality and preaching are not contradictory activities! Perhaps one leads to the other. However, my selection of Sheen as a parallel to Harris entails more than the preachy parallel between intellectuals.

Compared to Harris' neurological knowledge Bishop Sheen was quite obviously limited and seriously outdated. What has moved me to include Sheen is that, before he goes off into the preachy realm of helpful wisdom (and that realm is being duplicated by Harris), he reflects upon what is science, what is the domain and hence any limits of science, what is the relation of philosophy and religion and what is the relation between philosophy and science. I find a dearth of such theoretical pre-reflection in the works of Harris thus far consulted. Maybe Harris has reached the deepest profundity in such abstractions, but, alas, I do not have access to any such written evidence thereof. I will, however, not follow Sheen's Aristotelian-Thomistic thinking, rather initiate my own peculiar path. The comparison between Sheen and Harris evinces a sameness between apparent opposites.

The Task: I shall in ensuing sections consider the fundamental contradiction in the argumentation of Harris, a cross(way) Harris must bear, if intellectual honesty is to be observed. Certainly, a contradiction in theory constitutes a fragile basis for systematic consistency. Beyond that, I shall briefly take up a few derivative difficulties in Harris' argumentative thinking. I am endeavoring with this study to imitate the conciseness of Harris as evidenced in the limited number of pages of his book, all of which forces me to compress argumentation to the minimum of length. Harris' failure to include philosophical reflections has allowed him to "rationally" proceed at times in a paradoxically irrational manner. However, before taking up a critique it is first necessary to enter into Harris' freethinking about "free will"

Preaching the "Good News" Harris Reveals: «Free Will Is An Illusion»

Harris' analysis and evaluation of free will contains three levels. First of all, he presents the theoretical reasons, grounded in the determinism of science, that compel him to judge *truly* that there is no free will, that free will is but an illusion. Secondly, striking contentions are asserted explicitly formulating this rejection, indeed, even contending that any interpretation of free will is simply incoherent. And thirdly, short exemplary discussions are undertaken to illustrate the meaning of the rejection. For example, Harris explicitly and forcefully demises notions such as "sin" and "retributive justice", indeed, as effectively morally objectionable (cf. pp. 49-63). Such notions are dependent upon free will and, hence, false with pernicious effects. Levels two and three are not radically separated from each other. Let us now turn to the premises of Harris' argumentation.

Harris' commitment to a fully deterministic notion of science constitutes *the* presumption underlying all his assertions on free will. Harris is aware that many people, based upon their own self-experience, think that they have free will. Harris simply vitiates such deceptive feelings of freedom. Unfortunately, so Harris, such feelings often lead people falsely to think that the apparently firsthand awareness truly reveals to the self the self's freedom. So, Harris addressing the plethora of deluded believers, now informed of the "scientific" truth, writes:

> You would, of course, continue to feel free in every present moment, but the fact that someone else [i.e., the scientist] could report what you were about to think and do would expose this feeling for what it is: an *illusion*. If the laws of nature do not strike most of us as incompatible with free will, that is because we have not imagined how human behavior would appear if all cause-and-effect relationships were understood (*FW*, 11).

The laws of nature ordain evidently a strict, unremitting, all-encompassing, pitiless and asymmetrical "cause-and-effect" relationship. What does such a relationship signify for the mind's supposed "freedom"?

> There is no question (most [?], if not all) mental events are the product of physical events. The brain is a physical system, entirely beholden to the laws of nature—and there is every reason to believe that changes in its functional and material structure *entirely dictates* our thoughts and actions (*FW*, 11-12). (*Italics* and stress added.)

This means of course that the very brain that causes the effects constituting Harris' thinking has "entirely dictated" each and every word, the specific ordering of words as sentences and the meaning expressed that Harris, the *"free*thinker"[6], has been thinking. For that matter, the reader's brain also dictatorially imposes upon the reader's own intellect whatever interpretation of Harris's words that his/her thinking mind might believe to have understood. Bluntly put, the brain "entirely dictates" what Harris himself thinks he meant with his thought about the brain's causal power that entirely determines what he is thinking. Correspondingly, the reader, using his own (sic) intellect, understands nothing on his own because his ideas are not his own (*qua* autonomy), rather they have been *entirely* (i.e., completely, totally, fully) *dictated* (i.e., transmitted, ordained, imposed) by a biological factor external in some still unknown way to consciousness, a thing of nature that just happens to bear the colloquial name of "brain". Evaluating Harris' thesis, I feel constrained to conclude that the brain, because it *entirely dictates* what humans think, want and do, can rightly be designated as a *totalitarian dictator*, relative to which everyman's conscious intellect is *nothing else other than* a mere abject subject because lacking all autonomy. Whatever noble or abominable thoughts might occur, they are entirely imposed. The totality of *my* mind (or *your* conscious mind too, dear reader) with all its thoughts, values, volitions, decisions and activities are *naught but* an illusion, and nothing more. This dubious illusion derives from the belief that the mental events called the thinking of my own conscious mind are really mine, that they really express my *own* autonomy. They do not! Science has spoken! Let darkness engulf the autonomous intellect in a vail of causal heteronomy. That is *the* theoretical *waking* preached by Harris!

Now to the theory in its concrete formulations: What is the indubitable law forming and informing Harris' reasoning? The iron dictates of the cause-and-effect connection is the answer. Harris allocates but a few pages (*FW*, pp. 8-11) to the theoretical foundation. For instance, Harris asserts that Benjamin Libet has shown that:

> [A]ctivity in the brain's motor cortex can be detected some 300 milliseconds before a person feels that he has decide to move. [Other] experimenters found two brain regions contained information which button subjects would press a full *7 to 10 seconds* was consciously made. More recently, directed recordings from the cortex show that the activity of merely 256 neurons were sufficient to predict 80 percent accuracy a person's decision to move 700 milliseconds before he became aware of it (*FW*,8-9).

Harris' reductionist conclusion crescendos in factual certainty:

> One fact now seems indisputable. Some moments before you are aware of what you will do next—a time in which you subjectively appear to have complete freedom to behave however you please—your brain has already determined what you will do [and I, the author of this study, add whatever you, dear reader, will consciously or happen to think]. You then become conscious of this "decision" and you believe that you are in the process of making it ... There will always be some delay between the first neurophysiological events that kindle my next conscious thought and the thought itself (*FW*, 9).

Harris seems quite confident that his reader will make the right cognitive "decision", namely that Harris has proved his point. And the point is: Whatever "decision" of any type (be it to eat or not, or to buy a book or not, or *to decide* that

Harris is right or not, or etc. *ad infinitum*) is ultimately *not anything else other than* a product of the brain, and an illusionary concoction at that, i.e., particularly if a person claims to be making an autonomous decision. The reason offered by Harris for this thesis derives from a rather perfunctory understanding of time as an asymmetrical flowing from past to future, within which, if event-A is causally related to event-B, then event-A will appear at present point t^1 to be followed later by event-B, so to speak, downstream at new present point t^2. The temporal interval between point t^1 and t^2 has been shown to be so tiny as 700 milliseconds or even 300 milliseconds. The number of milliseconds, however, is not the principle here, rather it is that *any* amount of time flow, be it only one-half of 1 millisecond (or even less) or seven thousand milliseconds (or more), is of no importance. What alone counts for Harris is the asymmetrical interval of time itself that connects events together in a causal relationship[8].

Harris does not speculate at all just how much temporal duration that event-A (or event-B) might need in order to enjoy its own present existence in a given "now". If any temporal location "*t*" is viewed as just a point in time, then there was not even an event because a temporal point must have durational width, thereby annihilating the duration of the event's temporal being. Furthermore: No consideration is spent thinking about how the successive on-goings within the event itself are causally related. For after all, events are durational such that the changing elements of the durational "now" can evince causality emanating from a later element that retroactively alters fundamentally a previous element of the event sequence. What is of importance at this moment, moreover, is that the reader become fully aware of the *reductionism* structuring the formulations made by Harris or, better, those ideas antecedently caused by his brain, presuming of course that his own brain is really doing its own computing and is not being duped by a super brain secretly determining his own brain to think the thoughts it does—and this is no frivolous concern as we shall see.

I will let Harris sum up matters once again;

> You are not in control of your mind—because you, as a conscious agent, are only *part* of your mind, living at mercy of other parts [e.g., the brain] (*FW*, 37-38).

> All our behavior can be traced to biological events about which we have no conscious knowledge: this has always suggested that free will is an illusion (*ML*, 136).

> The problem is that no account of causality leaves room for free will (*ML*, 138).

Everything we take ourselves to be at the level of our subjectivity—our memories and emotions, our capacity for language, the very thoughts and impulses that give rise to our behavior—depends upon distinct processes that are spread out over the whole of the brain (*WU*, 205)

By far the most of what Harris writes is concerned with what a preacher might want to spread as "good news". It is just that in Harris' case such a gospel finds its scripture in the text entirely "written" by the brain or, provocatively formulated: It is a matter of material over mind. An example of Harris' preaching can be seen in his decided rejection of sin and moral responsibility. There is no sin and no moral responsibility (where free will plays a role) in nature's cosmos. For Harris, such libertinism is liberating:

Losing a belief in free will has not made me fatalistic—in fact, it has increased my feelings of freedom. My hopes, fears, and neuroses seem less personal and indelible (*FW*, 46).

I hesitate to explain why the loss of free will is the producer of freedom, i.e., unless freedom means being freed the obligations of moral imperatives, either from God (Christianity/Islam) or from reason (cf. Immanuel Kant). For instance, Harris resolves the ancient problem concerning the crime of regicide (extendable, I hold, to presidents such as Lincoln or, perhaps, nowadays to Trump[?]) in the following manner: Speaking to a hypothetical person who has diligently reflected on the matter of regicide and who has finally decided (really?) to assassinate the king, Harris writes:

… [W]ell, then killing the king reflects the sort of person you really are. The point is not that you are the ultimate and independent cause of your actions; the point is that, for whatever reason, you have the mind of a regicide (*FW*, 52-53).

It is personally unfortunate for John Wilkes Booth that he did not know that line of argument, particularly before Lincoln's contemporaries shot him dead. That retributive execution was all so unfair to Booth (but not unjust as there is no justice in a world absence of free will), because he could do nothing else, his mind being, well, one of a presidentcide. But then, his shooters had the mind of a "shoot 'em-dead-cide". Moral guilt, not to speak of sin, is absent from Harris' world view. However, judicial farces remain as seen in the attempt of the Nurnberg Trials retributively to assign responsibility for genocide. Enough of preacher Harris, the point has been reached to commence my critique of theorist Harris.

The Hermeneutics Guiding Criticism

I hereby return to the theoretical examination of Harris' argumentation. I hope that it is clear to my reader that the presupposition to Harris' reductionist argument concerning the conscious mind and the brain. Reductionism can have various general formulations. For instance: 1. *B is nothing but A* or 2. *B is not anything else than A* or 3. *B cannot be anything other than A.* In all formulations given, the reduction is due to the fact that B has no real being in itself, rather it is a function of the being of A, conceived here as factor-X, i.e., a factor external to and casually determining B. It is really so, argues Harris, that *autonomous* thinking is *nothing but, not anything else than*, or *cannot be anything other than* the unconscious machinations of the X-factor, here the brain. Conscious autonomy is thereby reduced *to nothing but* heteronomy.

It is Harris' radical *reductionism* that constitutes the cognitive cross upon which I shall gleefully nail the integrity of his argumentation. This, the resultant crossway of my critique, will require Harris to make a cognitive decision between two alternatives in order to maintain either rationality or consistency of theory. The twain does not meet. Whatever decision Harris will make, his theory falsifies itself. The cognitive snake will dine on a succulent feast of self-immolation. In order to present my critique, I find it advisable to pause a bit to reflect some upon the structure of reductionism. Harris himself has not formalized his reductionism. But a fellow materialist has, name Karl Marx. Let us check Marx' formalization of reductionism.

The young Marx forcefully contended in the *German Ideology* (1845/46)[9]:

> Morality, religion, metaphysics and other ideology and the *forms of consciousness* corresponding to them retain herewith no longer the appearance of independence. They have no history, they have no development ... (MW, 26-27). (*Italic* added)

Personally, I own several histories of Western philosophy written by fine historians such as Nicolas Abbagnano/Giovanni Fornero, Friedrich Copelston, Guillermo Fraile/Teófilo Urdánoz, Hermann Schmitz and Wilhelm Windelband[10]. If Marx is to be believed, the different philosophies presented in the various histories are in no way genuine products of the conscious mind of each philosopher, rather they possess in reality *no* history, evince *no* real development. This is stunning! (Also, it means that the money used to purchase said histories was a waste of resources.) But the hard fact is that Marx the materialist did, indeed, most emphatically contend that there is no longer (and effectively that there never was in the past) any historical development of philosophy because the very thinking that consciously philosophizes do has *no* "independence" (viz., "autonomy") in itself.

14

Something beyond or outside of the philosophizing mind has caused the chronicle of philosophies. In the terms of Harris, the theoretical "forms of consciousness" constituting philosophy are nothing other than an *illusion*. Retuning the Harris' vocabulary, the brain has evidently played tricks on those historians who falsely thought they had been chronicling the real development of philosophy through the ages. Sad, so sad, not to speak of being ecologically wasteful of the paper expended for their books.

What reason could Marx possibly advance in order to justify his denying of independence (or autonomy) to the rational thinking that produces morality, religion, metaphysis and other types of theory? Unlike Harris the materialist, Marx the materialist does clearly announce the foundation of his materialism for all the world to read. In *Die Deutsche Ideologie* Marx tears away all veils concealing the determining depths of human consciousness:

> Consciousness [Bewußtsein = {having-become-knowing-being}] *cannot be anything other than* being having-become-conscious being [bewußtes Sein], and the being [Sein] of humans is their real-life process (*MW*, 26). (*Italics* added)

> It is not consciousness that determines life, rather it is life that determines consciousness [= being-having-become-conscious] (MW, 27)[11].

Very briefly, I will attempt to render comprehensible what Marx' (and consequently Harris') *reductionism* means. Let us imagine that person-B arrives in his hometown from abroad. He wears the very worn and tattered garb of a priest, Catholic or Anglican, and says that he is returning temporarily from the poverty belts of Africa where he tends to the disparate needs of his impoverished flock, an isolated tribe. Hunger and sickness reign there – and the cleric's considerable rhetorical skills describes with vivid and heart-ringing detail the history of how the tribe has been marginalized, neglected and exploited despite his best efforts. With a preaching, vibrant with the desire to return to his flock, the priest beguiles and inspires various audiences "freely" to give lots of money to be used by the priest upon returning to his suffering flock. Person-B, the priest, is successful beyond his wildest hopes. Charity flows in exuberance. Finally, running out of further groups to beguile, the priest ends his preaching and goes the next day with the money to the bank and deposits this monetary collection to his private hidden account in the Fiji Islands, buys a plane ticket for himself and his "husband", the two taking off the next day for a life of debauchery luxuriating in the Fiji Islands.

It thereby becomes clear that the person-B as a caring priest *is nothing but, cannot be anything other than* a swindler, a fraud, whom I shall call person-A. The history of the actions of person- B *qua* being a priest is an illusion, i.e., it cannot be anything other than the dynamics of a swindler, viz. person-A. In other words, the thoughts, wishes, willing and acts of deciding carried out by person-B is no more than a "direct outflow" or "direct discharge" from the real intentions of the confidence man, person-A (= factor-X). Bluntly stated, B is clearly nothing but A in the form of a semblance of charity. The conscious thinking, volitions and acts of deciding of person-B are nothing but an *illusion* in Harris' terms. In itself, there is nothing contradictory in any proposed reduction, i.e., so long as the scope of the reduction does not ascribe its strictures to a class of people that includes the reductionist himself. Such self-reference can swiftly stoke the cognitive snake to feast upon itself. The reductionist must not be included in his own asserted reduction or he forfeits his claims to rational thinking. As it stands, *Harris along with Marx belongs to the very class of persons affected by the reduction, a situation in which what is asserted in the theory as true, does not logically permit the one asserting to affirm as true the theory enunciated.* In what way does the reductionism of Harris jeopardizes the truth value of his consciously asserted denial of autonomy to human consciousness? Alas, the truth of Harris's ideas is also their falsification, thereby leaving Harris at a cognitive crossway.

Harris strikes me as a highly intelligent person who earnestly *desires* to know the truth about just what constitutes the relationship between the brain and "consciousness", who *actively* chose to study profoundly the matter, developed his ideas, organized his thoughts into a system and, then tested their adequacy of scope and explanatory power, and finally *volitionally* examined closely their cognitive agreement with (or correspondence to) the way mental and biological reality truly interact. Summarizing Aristotle, Mortimer J. Adler notes something implicitly valid for Harris: namely that "thinking truly consists in an agreement between what one thinks and what one is thinking about"[12].

To the truth of that he is thinking, Harris emphatically lends his assent. In summary: *Harris has seemingly uncovered theoretically the "how" of the way things neurologically are and knows that his theory corresponds truly to the way things are.* Based on the methodological framework leading to this knowledge, Harris develops his further analyses in various books. And, I repeat, he effectively treats that framework as apodictic, viz., certain beyond reasonable doubt. Surely, the *truth* of his reductionist foundation is of supreme importance for Harris as it grounds his preaching that is often sincerely solicitous for serious human problems. The next question is: Does Harris' foundational reductionism permit truth assertions at all?

Criticism

Examining Harris in terms of truth. I accept the traditional formulation of what truth is, I have briefly examined the definition of what truth is, namely a correspondence of theory, viz., *conformitas vel adequatio intellectus ad rem*. But I must go beyond this formal definition, which only defines "what truth is", but does not reveal the very "being of truth"[13]. Truth cannot be adequately understood simply as an objective declarative proposition appearing to the conscious intellect. The judgment that a given intelligible content of proposition X^1 corresponds truly to the structural reality of X presents just a statement announcing an "égalité logique"[14] between X^1 and X called truth. This equality is not, however, the "being of truth" (or "esse *veritatis*") in the conscious subject *qua* judging truth. More is needed, and this more is an act of *assenting to*, viz., *internally appropriating* said content into the very reality of the subject's mental being, viz., *infusing* the truth content into one's intellectual and volitional self. In a sense, the subject must become truth and truth must become the subject. In other words, once assenting, one's self-identity becomes informed by the truth. I shall explain myself briefly.

The conceptualization of object-X can be used as the means for knowing said object-X, i.e., the thinker can compare the conception with object-X as so conceived in order to determine if the asserted conformity is valid or not. The act of such a comparison and determination of validity is precisely the act of judging, which in positive cases results in a declaration of "truth" about reality *as it really is*. One more feature, however, is necessary to generate the "being/*esse*" of truth as a reality residing in the consciousness of the thinking subject. What has been said about correspondence is the *sine qua non* for the becoming to be of truth, but not yet generative of its "being" actual in the mind. By means of the *intellect's volitionally undertaken act* of *judging* the conformity, a moral like imperative confronts the judging subject demanding him or her *to recognize, acknowledge and, most importantly*, to *submit the intellect to* the *truth proposed*. As the philosopher, Walter T. Stace, correctly noted long ago:

> Both the given and the laws of logic are absolute, are forced upon us *ab extra*, whether we like it or not, whether it suits our convenience or no. … Truth, therefore, is not whatever we will to believe. … Truth is compelled both by facts and by logic[15].

Truth gains its being/*esse* in the reality of the thinking subject by means of the intellect's *freely* assenting to the truth claimed. Truth as objectivity to be appropriated compels conformity upon the intellect true to itself. It is the free will of the free intellect that decides to assent to a proposition as true, "whether it suits our convenience of no". Truth comes to be when the structural dynamics of reason, seeking to understand the what, how or why of things as they really are, volitionally submits, viz., rationally wills to affirm reason's dictates. It is the act of reasoning, free from a factor-X, that "dictates" the conformity that the intellect *willingly* assents. In other words, whereas the judgment derives from the force of reasoning, the assent transforms the reasoned belief into a *responsibly* taken decision to believe the truth as the subject's reality. With that act of a volitional submission (= act of free reason's free will) truth is appropriated and internalized by the judging subject into the self's autonomous responsibility. Failure mentally to conform, despite insight, is experienced, so noted, as compulsion upon the will by the nature of things as they are. A judgment of conformity *assented to by the intellectual will* produces the *freedom* of understanding.

By using the terms "free" or "freedom", I mean that the structural dynamics of the intellect function unrestrained by any factor-X, a factor which supposedly *entirely dictates* to the mind's intellect what it will feel, think, judge and hold for true. It is precisely the *free* intellect that Harris, applying reductionism, must and does call an *illusion*. If the intellect is not free, then the will cannot be free. Hence, Harris validly rejects free will because free reasoning power itself cannot be anything else than an illusion. The unintended consequence is that Harris' own theory prohibits him from validly applying his "rational" reduction to his *own* mind. His ideas, just like those of anyone else, are entirely dictated to him and any ideas of evaluation of their truth, also, are naught but a dictation from factor-X. In contrast, the "FREE will", as I am contending, is a function of "FREE reason". Reasoning entails both cognitive *desiring* and rational *willing*. Cognitive reasoning can only function if it is autonomous, i.e., if it is adequately *free from* external factor-X's so as to be able to operate unconstrained by said influence. "Freedom" thereby means that the actively, intentionally and volitionally investigating intellect is liberated from being determining causally by any factor-X. Harris' reductionism means that he cannot on principle use his own rationality because any rational justification is supposedly *nothing other than* a biologically caused *illusion*. Harris' mind possesses *per* theory no autonomy and, therefore, has no freedom *in toto* from external determinism. This situation is fatal to Harris's rejection of free will.

What a dilemma! If Harris claims to be consciously reasoning, then the universality of his reductionism collapses. If Harris sticks to his reductionism, he then forfeits the mental autonomy that allows thinking rationally and freely to assent to his theory as truth. Harris cannot, thereby, keep his mind as his own because of his reductionist theory negates any "own" to be kept. Directly stated: his autonomous reason is nothing else other than an illusion! Consequently, he loses his (rational) mind and has no permissible argument.

I suspect that Harris, should he become conscious of the dilemma, would remain doggedly with his reductionist reasoning and forcefully claim that those who seek a causation other than physical (asymmetrical) causation "invoke a metaphysical entity, such as the soul, as the vehicle for our freely acting wills" (FW, 16). Along with such a terminological scoff, Harris would probably respond by doubling down even deeper into his physicalist reductionism, which he effectively does a few lines further down the text:

> Unconscious neural events *determine our thoughts and actions*—and are themselves determined by prior causes of which we are subjectively unaware (*FW*, 16). (*Italics* added)

Holding on to the neurophysiology of human thought and behavior, Harris apodictically asserts, "we can no longer locate a plausible hook upon which to hang our notions of personal responsibility" (WF, 17). Contrary to Harris, I suggest that my presentation of *free* will as a function of *free* reason could well serve as "the hook" upon which to hang *volitional* autonomy and, hence, moral responsibility[16]. Harris quotes J. Greene & J. Cohen writing that the view of people believing in free will "requires the rejection of determinism and an implicit commitment to some kind of magical mental causality …" (*FW*, 74). The inclusion of the adjective "magical" boarders on cheap propaganda. No one seriously argues for free will as a "magical" power. However, the fact that there is causality different from the physical causality, namely reasoning itself constituting a *mental* causality FREE from factor-X, is worthy of examination. Hence, I shall finish this study by briefly expounding a limited description of the *mental causality* proper to the initiation of reasoning and willing. Examinations of "mental causality" constitute no rarity. Arthur C. Danto dedicated a chapter to the subject in his book on basic concepts of philosophy[17]. Whether the free intellect constitutes ontologically immaterialism, representational materialism or identity fusion is irrelevant to the ensuing discussion of the intellect's mental causality proper[18]. The only prerequisite is that the theorist at least accepts "that we *cannot* think conceptually *without* our brains, but that we *do not think* conceptually *with* our brains"[19]. I do not intend to treat "mental causality" in its breath. That is beyond my powers. Instead I will sharply focus upon the initiating causality of freely reasoning and freely choosing. I will take my lead from Bernard J. F. Lonergan's study of human understanding[20]. The product of the intellect's pursuit of truth is understanding something about the world as is.

The Mental Causality of Understanding as Fact

Thoroughly understand what it is to understand and not only will you understand the broad lines of all there is to be understood but also you will

> possess a fixed base, an invariant pattern, opening upon all further developments of understanding (*ISHU*, xxviii).

The *factual* reality that is experienced understanding arises through a fusion of both its efficient cause (motivation) and final cause (purpose). This "fact" reflects the mind's primordial subjectivity, namely that the intellect continually seeks a "Why?" for his world.

> Where does the 'Why?' come from? What does it reveal or represent? ... It is that tension, that drive, that desire to understand, that constitutes the primordial 'Why?'. Name it what you please, intellectually inquiry, active intelligence, the drive to know. ...
>
> This primordial drive, then, is the pure question. It is prior to any insights, any concepts, any words, for insights, concepts, words, have to do with answers; and before we look for answers, we want them; such wanting is the "Why?" Name it what you please, alertness of mind, intellectual curiosity, the spirit of inquiry, active intelligence, the drive to know (*ISHU*, 9)-

The primordial "Why?" seeks answers granting understanding, the absence of which causes this drive to be felt as a tension that generates the mental energy motivating resolution. This is the "primordial" causality of mind's desire to know.

> Deep within us all, when the noise of other appetites is stilled, there is a drive to know, to understand, to see why, to discover the reason, to find the cause, to explain. ... It can absorb a man (*ISHU*, 4).

Lonergan explicitly distinguishes this mental causality from biological necessities.

> The first movement is an awakening of one's intelligence [intellect]. It is release from the dominance of biological drive and from the routines of everyday life. It is the effect emergence of wonder, of the desire to understand (*ISHU*, 10).

This particular tension constitutes the psychological energy driving the intellect's searching for truth as a response to the "Why?" (or the "How?" or the "What?") of things as they are. Here is the function of "insight" as the entrance into rationality.

> [I]nsight comes as a release from the tension of inquiry (*ISHU*, 4).

As an example of "insight", Lonergan uses the story of Archimedes who was asked by King Hiero to find a way to discern whether a crown was really made of gold or of added baser materials. Archimedes suddenly grasped the solution. Weigh the crown in water and observe the displacement. Archimedes had discovered what has become to be called the principle of specific gravity. In his exuberance, Archimedes spontaneously scurried naked from the baths of Syracuse with a vibrant cry of insight: "Eureka".

> What better symbol could one find for this obscure, exigent, imperious drive, than a man, naked running, excitedly crying 'I've got it' (*ISHU*, 4).

Insight releases the intellect's tension of inquiry by generating rational penetration into the intelligible nature of a puzzling problem! This mental reward, experienced psychologically by the excited Greek, is precisely incipient "understanding". A seeker of truth cannot do otherwise that assent to the truth found. An insight presents to the seeker of knowledge a "clue" that can be articulated in to systematic knowledge. The release from cognitive tension moves the intellect willingly to affirm and freely to assent to the articulated insight as revealing truth. The process of articulation has been well described by Stephen Pepper.

> A man desiring to understand the world looks about for a clue to its comprehension. He pitches upon some area of common sense fact and tries if he cannot understand other areas in terms of this one. ... A list of its structural characteristics becomes his basic concepts of explanation and description. We call them a set of categories. ... He undertakes to interpret all facts in terms of these categories[21].

In my criticism of Harris's argumentation, I sought to show that the rational thinking necessitates the autonomy of mental causality, not its helpless subservience to factor-X. This is a direct refutation of Harris' reductionism of mental events to being nothing but a function of brain causality. If Harris does not accept my reasoning, then he forfeits his own ability to reason against me, being that the mental causality of his reasoning is then nothing but an illusion. Immediately above I have described, following Lonergan, the primordial origins of thinking rationally. I, surreptitiously, introduced the claim that my analysis of mental causality constitutes a "fact", indeed, a "subjective fact". My assertion of factuality reveals the total divide between my methodology and that of Harris' one-sided scientism. This assertion I will briefly explain availing myself of the "new" phenomenology of Hermann Schimtz[22].

According to Schmitz, the positive sciences (and I think here of neurology) search for objective facts. A fact is *objective*, if every and anyone with sufficient knowledge and language proficiency can make a statement about the content held to be factual. If Schmitz is sad, then any sociologist, psychologist or neurologist can describe observable and confirmable features of Schmitz, including his brain activity. On the other hand, a fact is *subjective*, if only one person, namely the one who makes assertion, can experience it and express it with sufficient linguistic proficiency. In other words, Schmitz, and Schmitz *alone*, can describe the factual structure of his self-experience of being sad. Schmitz alone can focus upon his "I am sad", i.e., subjective experience. And this Schmitz does in his 9 volume, 5000+ page *System der Philosophie*. It is exactly self-experience that Harris impugns as "illusion", forgetting that the very process of the specific reasoning to this conclusion is his own reasoning and, hence, open to the same debunking. Above I argued ostensibly in favor of the autonomy of the mental causality called the intellect's reasoning. In truth, I possess in fact only one single example of autonomy directly to describe and that is my own. When Lonergan writes: "A man desiring …", I, the author of this essay, am *that* man and I say: "I desire to understand …". The dilemma that I have laid at Harris' feet, is one that concerns *me* directly in my uniqueness. Harris, in accordance with a method of objective fact finding, denies that I factually do possess my "own" subjectivity at all. I am quite willing to accept the possibility that Harris is nothing else other than a biological automat that has accidentally spurted out rationally organized ideas that a capricious brain has projected into his consciousness. I do not, however, accept this assumption for myself. Period! The description of insight given by Lonergran is first and foremost a depiction of what I, Leonard Wessell, directly experience as my *own* unique experience, i.e., as a *subjective* fact, and facts cannot be omitted if a thinker wants to understand himself and his world. And I do accept *subjective* fact[23].

Harris' objective thinking is, I contend, the product of centuries of sensualistic introjectionism and physiologism, which projects an "outer" realm called the world that is separated from the "inner" realm in which consciousness is encased. In one way or another the "outer" has to be filtered through some medium into the "inner", which in the case of Harris is the task of the brain (for which he mistakenly thinks he has *direct* and *non-mediadated* evidence)[24]. An explanation of this thesis requires another article. At this point, I will end my dispute leaving my reader with "Fichte's choice"[24]. In his *Science of Knowledge* (1794) Fichte admits that a realist of his day can construct a perfectly coherent argument for his "dogmatism". At the same time, Fichte claims an equal validity for his idealism. One side could not rationally refute the other, thus Fichte. So, Fichte left the final decision of truth to his reader, up to the kind of character the reader had. Harris has presented a perfectly coherent argument which, if one ignores the problem of applying to own self, seems solid. I hold that I have developed a coherent argument in favor of free reason and free will, one seemingly solid. So, I leave it up to the reader to decide. I know well my decision

Footnotes

1   Sam Harris, *Free Will*, New York: Free Press, 2012. All citations will be given in the text as *FW* + page number.

2   Prof. Mariano Álvarez Gómez has presented a book length lecture to the Real Academia de Ciencias Morales and Políticas of Spain in which, in a far broader sweep, the problem of free will, viz., liberty is discussed. *See El problema de la libertad ante la nueva escisión de la cultura*: Madrid, Real Academia de Ciencias Morales y Políticas, 2007. My study is limited just to the specifics of Harris' argumentation.

3   The books by Harris that are full of "wisdom" are *The Moral Landscape. How Science Can Determine Human Values*, London: Black Swan/Transworld Publishers, 2012 *and Waking Up. Search for Spirituality Without Religion*, London: Penguin Books, 2014, which will be referred to in the txt as *WU*, + page.

4   The tv series was *Life is worth Living Series*, 1953-1957, published by McGaw Hill and his book *Peace of the Soul* (1949). I have selected the title just given because Harris himself concerns himself analogously with such questions that concerned Sheen.

5   Sheen, *The Philosophy of Science*, Providence: Cluny Media, 2019 (originally 1934), *Religion Without God*, Providence: Cluny Media, 2019 and *God and Intelligence in Modern Philosophy*, Longams: Gren & Co, 1925.

6   So that my reader does not think that I am surreptitiously suggesting that Harris really believes in freedom as entailed in thinking, I note that he recommends in his epistle to *America as a Christian Nation*, Susan Jacoby' <u>Freethinkers</u> (underlying added to underline clearly Harris' willingness to append the attribute "free" to his type of thinking). See, Harris, *Letter to a Christian Nation,* New York: Vintage Books, 2008, p. 115. It seems fair that in some way Harris lays claim possessing "freedom" relative to his way of thinking.

7   Harris' views on the asymmetric nature of causality is nothing new. By 1843 John S. Mill could write: "We may define, therefore, the cause of a phenomenon to be the antecedent or concurrence of antecedents, on which it invariably and *unconditionally consequent*". See Mill, *A System of Logic. Ratiocinative and Inductive Principles of Evidence and of the Methods of Scientific Investigation,* Book, III, p. 331 (reprinted by Benedictine Classics, Oxford, 2011). If I accept Mill's thesis, a problem arises with the causality of the creation and positioning in the text of the above cited thesis by Mill. In my judgment, the "real" causality motivating Mill was *de facto* teleological. It was not the sentence before the citation that "caused" its positioning in the text, rather the grand

strategy organizing the text in a logical manner befitting a book on logic. Bluntly: Mill's declarative sentence itself as a "phenomenon" cannot be explained by the very principle that it proclaims. Instead it needs the energy (efficient cause) generated by a consciously direct strategy (final cause) determining its positioning in the presentation (formal cause) within the text (material cause). The limitation of causality to an asymmetrical direction simply cannot explain teleological activity, including the strategy freely chosen by Harris to write his work against free choice.

8   I am using the former East Germany edition accessible in internet. The work cited is: Die Deutsche Ideologie / German Ideologie, Karl Marx – Friedrich Engels Werke, Band 3, s. 5-530: Dietz Verlag, Berlin/DDR, 1969. I used my own translation because English versions do not always capture the meaning of Marx' German. Indeed, I am not satisfied with my own. The internet reference is: http://www.M|werke.de/me03_430.htm#|_|||_Apologetischer_Kommentar.Page numeration is from the German original and not the internet numeration.

9   Abbagnano/Fornero, Historia de la filosofía: Hora, 1994 (the original Italian, UTET, 1956ff), 4 Vols.; Copelston., A History of Philosophy, Image Books, 1997ff (originally 1962ff), 10 Vols.; Schmitz, Der Weg der europäischen Philosophie, Verlag Karl Alber, 2 Vols., and Fraile/Undánoz, Historia de la Filosofía, Bibliotec de Autores Cristianos, Biblioteca de Autores Cristianos, 1957ff., 8 Vols. and Windelband (with Heinz Heimsoeth as editor), Lehrbuch der Geschichte der Philosophie, J. C. B. Mohr, 1948. Despite the scholarship, the histories of philosophies mentioned are, following Marxist reductionism, neither histories nor records of development. Indeed, they are naught but "direct discharges" of economic conditions in which the historians themselves deterministically reflect. The effect of this reductionism is very destructive of "free" thinking, i.e., thinking "free" from the determinism of X-factors, which reduce "freedom" to an illusion.

10 The only empirical evidence that Marx ever really marshaled to justify and define his economic interpretation of "life" is found in a short sentence right to the point. "Eating and drinking lodging, clothing and other things belong to life. The first historical deed is thus the production of means satisfying these needs, the production of material life itself ...(is) the foundation of all history ..." (MW, 28). If a theorist, according to Marx, can grasp the economic situation, all thought as conscious forms will emerge as a "direct outflow" (MW, 26) of said situation. That's it! Later Marxists have managed to squeeze out volumes of theories from Marx' "other things", particularly with a reference to sex and the sexual structure of society which, I guess, has made Marxism sexy.

11 Adler, *Aristotle For Everybody. Difficult Thought Made Easy*: A Touchstone Book, 1997 (originally 1978), pp. 152-153. Clearly, my interpretation of Harris attributes to him an implicit correspondence theory of truth and, simultaneously, I am contending that my interpretation adequately corresponds to Harris' thinking as a variant of reductionism. I am both consciously using for my analysis and also affirming it for myself the truth definition of "ancient" logic, concisely given in a minor scholastic's teaching: "[V]eritas in cognoscendo vel *logica, quae definitur: conformitas vel adequatio intellectus ad rem.* Cf. Seb. Reinstadler, Elementa Philosophiae Scholasticae: Herder &Co, 1935, 6th ed., Vol. I, 318. Harris' theories have no value at all if one cannot say of them, to use a modern jargon, "It is true that so-and-so [Harris' proposed theory] if and only if so-and-so [is the way theorized]" or "It is false that so-and-so if and only if not so-and-so". (Cf. Jonathan Barnes discussion of the matter in his *Truth, etc., Six Lectures on Ancient Logic*: Clarendon Press, 2007, 64-74.) For a more mature discussion of correspondence truth as so defined above, I suggest a leading Spanish philosopher, Antonio Millán-Puelles, "Verdad del Conocimiento" in *Léxico Filosófico, RIA*LP, 2002 (originally 1984), 583-593. Not only "ancient" logic, but modern logic too holds that "every proposition in a formal context is either true or false". (Cf. Susanne K. Langer, *Introduction to Symbolic Logic*; Dover Publications, 1953, 90.) I have made this slight detour in epistemology in order *to stress most sincerely* that Harris is being taken *very seriously* by myself. I consider him to be a thinker earnestly making declarative assertions with enormous ramifications for the cultural life of humankind and that he firmly holds his theses to be true – and that is his theoretical undoing.

12 The notion of the "being of truth" (as opposed to "What is truth?") is derived from my article "The Being of Truth: Critical Reflections on Richard Rorty's Denial of Truth" in *Sino-Christian Studies*, no. 15 (2013), 59-99 and is integral to my form of "objective idealism". Only a very bare minimum of the article has been incorporated in current discussion of the being of truth. For a readable introduction to "objective idealism", see Vittorio Hösle, *Philosophiegeschicthe und objektiver Idealismus:* Beck'sche Reilhe, 1996, 13-36 and *Die Krise der Gegenwart und die Verantwortung der Philosophie*, Beck'sche Reihe, 1997. Both Hösle and myself share a common mentor in the person of the American idealist Josiah Royce. I have excluded arguing against Harris from an idealist point of view, though I would be quite willing to do so in another context.

13 I take the term from André Lelande's article "Égalité" in his *Vocabulaire technique et critique de la philosophie:* Quadrige/PUF, 17th edition, 1991 (original edition 1922), 270. Truth represents the point of juncture of the subjective and objective elements of what truth is and what its being is.

14 Stace, *The Theory of Knowledge and Existence*. Claredon Press, 1932, p. 435.

15 Harris' materialism treats the thinking of the intellect as a causal product of the brain, hence erasing any "hook" upon which to attach personal responsibility (flowing from free will). Apparently, such a hook would be the "metaphysical entity" called the "soul". If, however, one accepts that the causality of the intellect in actu possesses its own dynamics, then it is hard not to conclude that it is immaterial, which constitutes the "hook". This is exactly what Mortimer Adler did decades ago. I quote Adler:

> In antiquity, the word "soul" (In Greek, *psyche*; in Latin, *anima*) was used to signify whatever was in living organisms that makes them alive, active without being acted upon. ... [T]he soul gives man his distinctive power— that of the intellect and, with it, the power of conceptual thought, the power of judging and reasoning, the power of making free choices. ...

> [This power] is the very antithesis of matter. The spiritual is the immaterial. ... [W]hen it is held that there is something spiritual about man ..., some measure of immateriality must be found in man, and it is found in his possession of his [free] intellect and free will.

> See Adler, *Intellect. Mind Over Matter*: Macmillian Publishing Company, 1990, 10-11.

16 Danto, *Connections to the World. The Basic Concepts of Philosophy. With A New Preface:* University of California Press, 265-269.

17 For the differing ontological positions see accordingly Adler, *Intellect*,24-40; Danto, *Connections,* 243-48, 252-253, 267-69; and Stephen C. Pepper, *Concept and Quality, A World Hypothesis:* Open Court, 1966, 69-93.

18 Adler, *Intellect*, p. 47.

19 Lonergan, *Insight. A Study of Human Understanding*: Harper & Row, 1978 (originally 1958). All quotations will be cited in the text as *ISHU* + page number. I stress that I am only concern with a small part of Lonegran's 700+ pages dedicated to the subject matter.

20 Pepper, *World Hypotheses. A Study of Evidence*: University of California Press, 1970 (originally 1942), 90.

21 Schmitz, *Der unerschöpfliche Gegenstand. Grundzüge der Philosophie:* Bouvier Verlag, 1990.

22 For a discussion of the mischievous factors just noted, see Schmitz, *Der unerschöpfliche Gegenstand,* 16-27 along with Schmitz, *Neue Grundlagen der Erkenntnistheorie:* Bouvier Verlag, 1994, 1-17. The whole of Schmitz' phenomenology rests upon his criticism of Western epistemology.

23 For an insight into the specifics of "Fichte's choice", see Peter Suber, "A Case Study in Ad Hominem Arguments: Fichte's *Science of Knowledge*" in *Philosophy and Rhetoric*, (1990) Vol. 23, 12-42. The article has been reproduced in internet as: https://legacy.earlham.edu/~peters/writing/fichte.htm.

Bibliography

Abbagnano, Nicholás, and G. Fornero. *Historia de la Filosopfía.* 4 Vols. Barcelona: Hora, 1994.

Adler, Mortimer. *Intellect. Mind Over Matter.* New York: Macmillan Publishing company, 1990.

Álverez Gómez, Mariano. *El problema de la libertad ante la nueva escisión de la cultura.* Madrid: Real Academia de Ciencias Morales y Políticas, 2007.

Barnes, Jonathen. *Six Lectures on Ancient Logic.* Oxford: Claredon Press, 2007.

Copleston, Fredrick. *A History of Philosophy.* 10 Vols., New York: Image Books, 1997ff, originally 1962, ff.

Danto, Arthur C. *Connections to the World: The Basic Concepts of Philosophy.* Berkeley: University of California Press, 1989.

Fraile, Guillermo, and Teófilo Undanoz. *Historia de la Filosofía.* 8 Vols. Madrid: Bibliotheca de Autores Christanos, 1957ff.

Harris, Sam. *Free Will.* New York: Free Press 2012.

_____ , *Letter to a Christian Nation.* New York: Vintage Books, 2008.

_____ , *Moral Landscape*: *How Science Can Determine Human Value.* London: Transworld Publishers, 2012

_____ , *Waking Up*: *A Guide to Spirituality without Religion.* London: Penguin Books, 2014.

Hösele, Vittorio. *Die Krise der Gegenwart und die Verantwortung der Philosophie.* München: Beck, 1997.

_____ , Philosophiegeschichte und objektiver Idealismus. München: Beck, 1997.

Langer, Susanne K. *Introduction to Symbolic Logic.* Mineola, NY: Dover Publications, 1953.

Lelande, André. *Vocabulaire technique et critique de la philosophie.* Quadrige/PUF: 17th Edition. Paris: Presses Universitaires de France, 1991

Lonergan, Bernard. *Insight: A Study of Human Understanding.* New York: Harper & Row, 1978, originally 1958.

Marx, Karl, and Friedrich Engels. *Die deutsche Ideologie*

Mill, John S. *S System of Logic. Ratiocinative and Inductive Principles of Evidence and of the Methods of Scientific Investigation.* Oxford: Benedictine Classics, 2011, originally 1926.

Reinstadler, Seb. *Elementa Philosophiae Scholasticae.* 6th Edition, Band I. FREIBURG: HEDER & CO, 1935.

Pepper, Stephen C. *Concept and Quality. A world Hypothesis.* Chicago: Open Court, 1966.

Schmitz, Hermann. *Neue Grundlagen der Erkenntnistheorie.* Bonn: Bouvier Verlag, 1994. Bonn: Bouvier Verlag, 1994.

_____ , *Der unerschöpfliche Gegenstand*: *Grundzüge* der *Philosophie*. Bonn: Bouvier Verlag, 1990.

_____ , *Der Weg der europäischen Philosophie*. 2 Vols. Freiburg: Verlag Karl Alber, 2007.

Stace, W. T. *The Theory of Knowledge and Existence.* Oxford, UK: Claredon Press, 1992.

Suber, Peter. "A Case Study in Ad Hominem Arguments: Fichte's Science of Knowledge". *Philosophie and Rhetoric,* 23 (1990), 12-42.

Wessell, Leonard P. "The Being of Truth. Critical Reflections on Richard Rorty's Denial of Truth". *Sino-Christian Studies,* no. 15 (2013), 59-99.

Windelband, Wilhelm. *Lehrbuch der Geschichte er Philosophie.* Edited by Heinz Hiemsoeth. Tübingen: J.C:B: Mohr, 1948.

Chapter 2

The Being of Truth

Abstract

Since logical positivism Anglo-American philosophy has engaged in a relentless critique of correspondence truth, culminating in Richard Rorty's claim that the very nature of truth cannot be rationally ascertained. "Truth" is thereby banned from philosophy (and philosophy itself is banned from reason, reduced to a form of imaginative literature). Rorty's neopragmatism has introduced a total value relativism into the American polity excluding all principled norms from social policy in American. Normative values relative to heterosexuality, man-woman marriage, killing innocents (viz., abortion), etc. are being politically relativized by the governmental introduction of politically desired "'x-group's rights", etc. in place of natural law: This study aggressively confronts on a rational level Rorty's contention by regrounding the nature of correspondence truth in terms of Anglo-American idealism. The nature and structure of truth is ascertained and shown to be universal and eternal in validity. Rorty's counter contention has no logical coherence except in terms of the nature of truth and, hence, is self-destructive.

Key-words: Truth, Correspondence, Idealistic Structure, Universality, Eternity

I. Introduction

"Truth" has been and still is the object of severe criticism, indeed, effectively subject to deconstruction, certainly since the logical positivists entered the fray. In Michael Devitt's *Realism and Truth,* the author apodictically asserts: "It follows from my explanation of correspondence truth that the notion is in no way epistemic." Devitt then goes on to claim: "In sum, to hold to Correspondence Truth is to believe in a notion of truth that is not explained in terms of evidence." Devitt clearly rejects any "objective and mind-independent nature of that reality" to which correspondence truth is supposed to refer.1 In *Formal Ontology* Fred Sommers asserts: "Correspondence theories must inevitably fail to come up with a coherent notion of the objective relatum of correspondence."2 Such censures of "correspondence truth" are in many ways modest compared to the outright rejection of truth *per se* by Richard Rorty. In his *Philosophical Papers*, Rorty reveals the "truth" about truth, particularly conceived in terms of correspondence: "Nobody should ever try to specify the nature of truth," concluding then that "no theory of the nature of truth is possible"3 It is the intent of this study to specify the nature of truth. But first, how do I intend to attempt the apparently impossible?

I will let Rorty himself suggest the path to be followed. In his most notable book, *Philosophy and the Mirror of Nature*, Rorty presents what he takes as the way philosophers discuss the perennial problem of truth. These philosophers, according to Rorty, envision the problem in the following terms: "To know is to represent accurately what is outside the mind; so to understand the possibility and nature of knowledge is to understand the way in which the mind is able to construct such representations"4. Rorty has well stated what must be achieved for there to be truth as correspondence. Challenged by Rorty's conceptualization, I intend to show how the "mind" *de facto* formulates said "representations" of reality, which in turn can be evaluated as true or false. My methodology finds its inspiration in Josiah Royce's discussion of the problem in terms of error or, more accurately, how error is possible. I am referring, of course, to Royce's famous 1885 discussion of "the possibility of error" in his *The Religious Aspect of Philosophy*.[5] In my judgment, the current discussions of truth to which Rorty belongs have strikingly exemplified Royce's thesis, namely that error is possible - no, that error has become suffocatingly actual. Polemically formulated, Rorty is the high priest of the philosophical oxymoron that "the truth is that there is no truth!" It is for that reason that I have chosen his thinking as a worthy foil for my reflections. Paradoxically I will follow his imperative "to understand the way in which the mind is able to construct such representations" which constitute essential features of that which constitutes truth. In other words, truth will be examined relative 'to its very being (*esse*). In my opinion the critics of truth have totally failed not only to consider adequately what truth is, but even in the most sketchy manner to reflect upon the very being of truth.

I have effectively taken Rorty's description of how philosophers have historically represented truth as a challenge that will in turn mold my analysis. However, I must at the onset distance myself from Rorty's historical reflections. I am not at all interested in any historical reflections or their evaluations. In other words, just how philosophers approach truth is of no concern to me. It is solely the manner by means of which I approach the problematic that inspires the ensuing study. No one else's opinions other than my own will be immediately examined. So, the question presents itself as to just how and why I intend to separate myself from Rorty's "philosophers"? First I will explain how I will exclude the reflections of other philosophers. I will do this by enacting a methodological *solipsism*. In order to grasp the method that I am adopting, it is first necessary to examine what I understand by *solipsism*.

Let an expert define *solipsism*. Alain Lercher offers a typical definition in the following words:

> An attitude of the mind which, caricaturing idealism by pushing it to the extreme, conceives of no other reality than the thinking subject. Since I think, I exist; I am sure of that, but the world and other human beings are possibly nothing but representations of my mind, they have no existence beyond the images of my dreams. "There is nothing but I who exist!" There is no philosopher, properly speaking, that recommends such a conception, but one finds solipsistic tendencies among certain idealistic philosophers.[6]

This definition constitutes a caricature. Why? It is quite irritating to have *solipsism* ascribed solely as a logical extreme of idealism as it can be shown that a realist position can even lead to a "*solipsism* without a subject."[7] However, the "who's who" of those who display *solipsism* is of no interest to me. Of interest to me is ridding myself of the caricature propagated by the definition above. My notion of a "methodological *solipsism*" is derived from the Austrian idealist, Robert Reininger. In his magisterial study *Metaphysik der Wirklichkeit*, Reininger commences his philosophy with just such a methodology. I will let Reininger speak for himself:

> Self-reflection is reflection upon the fact that reality is experienced by "me." One can only reflect upon that which one experiences. For this reason, the beginning of philosophy is a type of methodological solipsism, which has nothing to do with the thesis that only I, as the thinker, exist alone. The thesis is valid for every thinker. It is fundamentally self-evident. Each thinker is a practical solipsist, for no one has otherwise philosophized except by means of his own particular consciousness and all infor-

mation and knowledge which he has obtained and taken over from "others" come under consideration only to the degree as they have become his.[8]

Let me ponder these words, for they reveal why I am enacting a *solipsism*. I do indeed have conversations with others. I put myself in accord with another person and at the same time he puts himself in accord with me. But at no point in my expedience have I had direct access to an immediate experience of said he as a non-mediated I. So Reininger is correct that, practically speaking, I think by means of my "own particular consciousness." It is just this personal "field of consciousness" that constitutes the location where I do reflect philosophically. Indeed, at no point are my philosophical reflections more intense than when I - imitating Descartes with his meditations - isolate myself from others and even from philosophical dialogue in order, so to speak, to "mull it over in my mind." Consequently I will be carrying out my considerations on truth by treating my field of consciousness as the sole focus toward which to direct my universe of discourse.[9] In short, it will be within my "field of consciousness" that I propose to initiate a defense of a correspondence theory of truth." In other words, I will describe "my field of consciousness" so as to uncover how I formulate, assert and confirm truth(s). My endeavor to describe my field of awareness obviously places me within the broad purview of phenomenology. I am not, however, seeking to emulate the phenomenological greats. In no way do I possess such phenomenological perspicacity. But, since I am the only guide for my methodological *solipsism*, I have certain privileges and I will have to suffice. My immediate goal is to elucidate descriptively the structural coordinates which lend theoretical content to the metaphor of "my field of consciousness." In said terms I shall first discuss the static topography and then the dynamic vectoriality of "the field of consciousness" proper to me.

II. The Static Topography of my Field of Consciousness

The title of my study is the being of truth. The definite article obscures a certain ambiguity that I will now seek to clear up by amplifying the needed distinction. Although an understanding of the being of truth is the telos of this essay, I have for the moment limited the discussion to my field of consciousness. I am not denying that truth pertains to that which is beyond my particular consciousness. I am only setting it aside so as to be able to investigate truth in "the" field of consciousness that belongs to me. In this phase of my discourse I am concerned with "the" being of truth, not simply the being of truth. Why the quotation marks? The quotation marks delimit the nature of truth sought to the field of consciousness that constitutes the range of my awareness. Even within this limitation, a fundamental distinction must be enacted. For instance, it is true that any approach to the problematic of "truth" is difficult. Without doubt the truth is that there are many and even contradictory theories of truth. That some philosophers do not even occupy themselves with the problematic is also true. What I have just done is to offer a variety of truths, each of which differs somewhat as to content. It seems evident that the variability of truths is potentially infinite. This heterogeneity of truths is stipulated by me as the materiality of truth.

Despite the ascertainment of the variability evident in different and diverging truths, I note that each case exhibits a common formality. In-each "it is true that ..." or "the truth is that ..." which qualifies the proposition being enunciated, there is a communal participation in "being" true that is valid for all asserted material truths. In other words, each "is" (although being disjunctively and differentially applied) structurally constitutes a specification of the assertion formally determined as true. It is precisely this formality that I am also endeavoring to highlight by means of the quotation marks. The materiality of truth or, better, of truths is not yet the object of my theoretical concerns. Nor is the formal structure of the truth valid *per se* beyond my particular consciousness of relevance to the immediately following. My immediate intent is to elucidate "the" truth as it is before my consciousness in its formality. The materiality of truths in my field of consciousness will serve the function of illuminating "the" formal structure of truth in my field of consciousness. However, I will show that my methodological *solipsism* is not self-sustaining, that is, it eventually, inexorably leads to the problem of the truth *per se*, that is, truth transcampal. At this stage, however, such thoughts are not relevant.

The ensuing analysis will follow roughly the procedure used by the Swiss philosopher Gerhard Huber.[11] Since Huber's analysis is in German and since at times the German language does not allow for a simple translation, the English equivalents chosen will indicate a certain constraint. The most striking feature of that which enters into my field of consciousness is its bright presentness. This technical term is my translation of Huber's Gegenwärtigkeit. Presentness certainly suggests a different metaphorical base than is the case with Gegenwärtigkeit.[12] It is the English base which must of necessity inform my reflections. However, there are sufficient parallels between the bases so as not to entail a distortion of Huber's meaning. Presentness should in no way be understood temporally; it has nothing to do with now as opposed to then.[13] The Latin root is *praeesse*: "to be before." That which enters into my field of consciousness is there before said consciousness, filling it with content. Although I am aware of an endless succession of different things, events, ideas, etc., the importance lies not in the richness of this materiality, rather in the formality common to all contents, namely the fact that contents manifest, show or present themselves. This manifesting, showing or presenting constitutes the very formality which grants appearance to that which is present before my particular awareness, viz., entering into my field of consciousness. Thus, presentness constitutes the formality of all that "appears" in my field of awareness, manifesting itself with imposition as being before my consciousness. My consciousness does not determine the there-ness of the contents present, rather it registers them as being in said field as that, which fills my range of awareness. and this registering is the very act that constitutes the formality of the consciousness that is my field. The contents simply donate themselves by imposing themselves upon my consciousness which makes present their being there. This thesis must be further developed.

The contents of my field simply present themselves, direct themselves, turn themselves *of and from themselves*. Huber refers to the presentness of things as being there *von sich* or *von sich her*. *Von sich* can be translated as "of itself". This translation stresses that the content is in its materiality other than the consciousness that is aware of said content. The content is of itself. Matters are not so forthright with the *von sich her*. The German adverb *her*, related to the English *here*, does not mean static location but rather implies a directionality toward the speaker as the frame of reference. The German term is similar in meaning to the antiquated English word "hither". According to Huber, that which presents itself by its very presentness (or *Gegenwärtigkeit*) is directed of itself toward a frame of reference, that is, toward the consciousness in whose field it enters. I have sought to recast the directionality of *von sich her* using the preposition from. That which is *hither* is from somewhere being directed or turned toward a specific frame of reference – in this case, my field of awareness. Whatever might be the real cause (extra consciousness) of the contents is irrelevant. The objects before my consciousness in presentness are simply being there from their own selfness. In summary, the being turned or directed toward consciousness of the contents constitutes a fundamental directionality of that which is other than consciousness, yet present to it. Simply put, presentness manifests itself as a *direction toward*. However, the *of and* from are not the sole features of presentness.

The manifoldness that imposes itself upon my consciousness is vivid, forceful, influential, often to the point that it seems to absorb the entire field into itself, easily letting me forget, neglect or lose awareness of a certain co-presence. This co-presence lurks in the background, forming a backdrop that can be thematized either by the force of circumstances or voluntarily. For example, if I inadvertently sit on a pin, I spontaneously shout: "Ouch, that hurts me!" Or I consciously continue my intellectual efforts to determine what the being of truth is, motivated by the perplexities forcing themselves reflectively upon me. Therefore, presentness of and from itself is equally a being present for or to me. For this reason, present-ness is not only a "showing itself from itself" but also a "showing itself to or for me"' The *me* of the "for me" is not necessarily a self-conscious I. Such an I differentiates itself and delimits itself against the background as, for example, in the reflective act of thematically focusing upon an object specifically selected by me. The *me* in everyday life activities remains in the shades of the field of consciousness. The immediate and direct capturing of that which is simply and merely there topographically in my field of consciousness can, perhaps, be terminologically expressed with Whitehead's notion of prehension.[14] Whatever the preferred term, the description of the static topography of my field of consciousness is by no means yet complete.

It is fundamental to emphasize that the *me* is not to be conceived of as inert receptivity as in the surface of a mirror (to borrow a term from Rorty). This *me* possesses its own proper directionality toward, that is, it manifests a "directing myself" or a "turning myself" of and from myself toward that which manifests itself from and of itself in presentness. In even more specific terms, the essence of said "directing myself toward" of and from myself evinces its own proper directionality in the form of "being aware of" or "conscious of,' however much this "being conscious" remains obscurely in the background. Without the "directing myself,' ("being conscious of"') there is no "presenting itself" made present, which results in the disappearance from the field of any content "of and from itself." Simply put, if I lose my consciousness, my methodological *solipsism* ceases to be. Consequently, in my field of consciousness the "of and from itself" and the "of and from myself" represent the two structural moments indivisibly constitutive of the one and the very same presentness which informs my field of consciousness. Summary definition: The static topography of my field of consciousness is constituted structurally by the "indivisible toward" of the bidirectionality of the "of and from itself" and of the "of and from myself."

III. The Dynamic Vectoriality of my Field of Consciousness

Within the confines of my field there is present more than an amorphous and undifferentiated vagueness. On the contrary, that which takes place in this field of consciousness is a constant and pulsating flow, always seemingly moving on. Such transitoriness reveals itself strikingly while distinct, different and varied "things" coagulate, crystalize or solidify in the field, and then metamorphose uninterruptedly into other and new configurations. However, all things present are structurally things of and from themselves. It is by means of such things of and from themselves that the "objects," indeed, "logical objects" of judgments, manifest themselves as candidates for assertions of truth. The "objects", precisely as they are (presenting themselves), constitute the foundation for "objectivity," one fundamental note of truth. Objectivity offers the object relative to which truth is predicated.

In order for truth to be, the mere presence or, better, the mere "being present" of the "object" is not sufficient. To be sure, it is a *sine qua non*. Yet it requires an indispensable complement: the "of and from me." In other words, things do not just present themselves by imposing themselves of and from themselves upon my field, rather I concurrently occupy myself with said things appropriating them consciously in their being there "of and from themselves for me." In this way the "toward" of things in presentness is made present by the "toward" of the "of and from me," taking possession of the "for me" of objects "of and from themselves." I direct myself or turn myself toward things present by focusing myself on them, thematizing aspects and marginalizing others, pursuing themes, concerns, including, for instance, the study now being expounded. Within this context I have not just traced a static topography between the "of and from itself" and the "of and from myself", rather I have outlined an energetic bidirectionalty as a dynamic vectoriality in which things communicate or present themselves being there of and from themselves for the me who is making them present. In other words, the "of and from myself" transforms itself into an act of grasping consciously or, simply put, making present the presentness of things "for me." Without the conscious act "of and from myself" the things of and from themselves ate not in my field of consciousness. For the moment this field is the only one permitted in my universe of discourse. By means of the apprehending act, the "of and from myself" differentiates itself from the merely topographic presentness in order to transform itself into the thinking and reflecting "subject," into a querying I, which seeks to determine by thought what the things of and from themselves are and then to pronounce some truth about them. The "of and from myself" establishes the foundation which engenders the reflective "I" which can say: "I judge that... is true." In this manner, there arises the beginnings of "subjectivity" which complement "objectivity" within the field of consciousness, resulting in the twin coordinates entailed in whatever articulation of "the" truth that might be made.

IV. Profundization of the Intellection of Things "of and from Themselves" by the "of and from Myself" or Objects by Subjects

Thus far I have centered my reflections upon the topographical and vectorial features of mere presentness *qua* merely being present, of course, before my field of consciousness. The center of attention has been upon the subjective and objective configuration that constitutes my field. There is more entailed, however. Terminologically I have written about "things" being present, manifest, given, etc.

that enter into my field of consciousness as having been made present. I have also made use of Whitehead's term prehension to designate the mere there-ness of the content as appropriated by consciousness. Whitehead himself treated prehension as an integral part of apprehension. I will now expand upon prehensive mereness entailed in the apprehending consciousness. In reality I do not just prehend "things" in general as present, rather specific contents of varied sorts. For instance, I look about in a classroom and see "faces," "chairs," "windows," etc. that is, I literally see prehensively/apprehensively different kinds of things embodying a variety of concrete contents. It is only by abstraction do I come upon being conscious of "things *per se.*" Concretely I not only grasp in my intellection the mere presentness of things but also said things in their intelligibility. I am not referring to acts of abstraction that consciously seek common features among different things, rather to the unreflective acts which realize themselves quite spontaneously. The contents of my apprehension are united intrinsically (both precognitively and cognitively) as present. This thesis must be exemplified. I turn my head about in a classroom and I see a blackboard cognitively grasped as such in immediacy. No abstraction is involved. None whatsoever. Perhaps one can say I perceive protoconceptually things that constitute, so to speak, the configured furniture of my field of consciousness without necessitating any abstractive act. Moreover, without co-capturing the intelligibility of things in the immediacy of experiencing something specifically in my field, my awareness is effectively blind. This means that it is not possible solely to prehend things as just merely and immediately present, rather each act of prehending something is simultaneously an act of proto-conceptual grasping, i.e., apprehending that something in its intelligibility. Both prehension and apprehension together constitute primordial intellection. Without the proto-conceptual (ap)-prehension of the intelligibility of each thing manifest in presentness, it is impossible to obtain an awareness of the manifested manifold in my field of consciousness. Concisely put: nothing could enter into said field because each "thing" would be without a "whatness". The consequence of mere prehension without apprehension, would be the impossibility of having a logical object to which a truth claim can be predicated. Presentness entails structurally apprehended intelligibility along with prehensive immediacy. I will forthwith seek briefly to explain what I mean by "intelligibility."

Intelligibility is the identity of each thing in intellection whose manifold includes a certain unity of difference which causes diversity to emerge and which presents this diverse manifold simultaneously in the co-pertinence of its unity. The intelligibility of the varying elements entails the property of contributing, each according to its own proper nature, to the synthetic unity that penetrates the manifold, making it into a totality. This is to say: intelligibility exhibits itself in the congruent and cooperate structure uniting the diversity into unity [15].

Allow me to give this abstract definition a relatively simple example. I find myself in a classroom in Germany. First, I shut my eyes, even pressing them tightly together. But only for a few seconds. By closing my eyes, I am seeking to enact a break with my previously ongoing stream of consciousness, so full of objects. Thereafter I abruptly open my eyes and glance quickly about simply directing my vision toward my surroundings. What enters into and takes possession of my field of consciousness? Well, I experience at first a flash of light with chaotically mixed contents, all without clear and sharp distinction. Then there follows quickly a focusing of my attention resulting in an individualization as certain things begin to stand out in their intelligibility. I now clearly see students sitting in seats within an auditorium, objects between which I begin ingenuously to thematize by selecting "faces" as that about which I quite spontaneously say: "I am seeing faces right now.' Such an enunciation is uncontrived if not automatic, void of all abstractive thinking. In no way does such an assertion imply necessarily nor suppose in any way that a predication of truth is consciously being made. I have done no more than to translate directly my non-reflective experience into verbal expression.

What is entailed here? It is clear that I have apprehended at least two different sorts of things, both of and from themselves, namely faces and seats. But, there is more. I have apprehended the two sorts of things being of and from themselves and, isochronally, being of diverse intelligibility. For this reason, I recognize immediately that I am being confronted with two different types of things. I am going to develop in outline this intelligibility by conceptualizing it with the intent to produce a definitional concept, say, of a face that is presenting itself in my field of consciousness. More importantly, with the definition established I will be able to commence a discourse about "the" being of truth in my solipsistic universe.

I focus upon faces and derive schematically the following definition: A human face, seen from the front side and in vertical position, entails (1) a vertical figure which possesses an oval shape (head), (2) two sites more or. less horizontally localized in the center of the oval (eyes), (3) starting between the eyes, a line of slight width descends (nose), (4) another horizontal line with an opening below the nose (mouth) and (5) possibly visible two accessories, one on each side of the oval (ears). All these features mentioned and their relations communicate intelligibility because all contribute to the structural unity of the totality constituting the face. In other words, a "face" manifests its intelligibility by exhibiting the congruence of the manifold diversity in its very facial unity. With this outline definition I now possess a working concept that enables me to understand reflectively a specific "thing of and from itself", namely a human face. The very process of conceptualization grounds the possibility of making enunciations about the objects in my universe of awareness. This process is a prerequisite for a determination of that which "the" truth is in its formality, that is, "the" very being of truth in my field of consciousness.

I let my vision pass from one face to another and, at the same time, I will communicate my judgment as to what I see. In the very moment of rapidly looking about I see faces of various ethnic origins, e.g., German, Italian, Mongolian, Fijian, Inuit, perhaps Martian. ... . Wait! I am looking about too rapidly. Do I really see being before me Germans, Fijians, or Intuits, not to speak of a science-fiction Martian? Surely something is not right here, indeed, quite false! At any rate, I consciously interrupt the ongoing flow of my comments and I, with full awareness, force myself to pause and to begin to reflect, deliberate or meditate about the "truth" of what I have being announcing. Or more accurately, I become intentionally aware of the judgments I am ingenuously making and am now reflectively considering if they all are really true. The very act of distancing myself from the ongoing flow of enunciations in order to realize a reflection upon their truth value transforms the vectorial "of and from myself" clearly into a thinking subject, a reflecting "I," that conscientiously seeks to determine the truth value of the materiality of the propositions aspiring to the formality of "being true." By means of conscientious reflection I, so to speak, delineate the "'territory" in my field of consciousness where I can seek out and investigate the nature of formally "being true."

V. The Being of "the" Truth in My Field of Consciousness

Let me repeat my central interest: The innumerable enunciations qualified by the addition of "it is true" evince a universal formality which, because it is necessarily structural, configures the nature of truth in its formal being. At this point I am conceiving this structure as the "being of truth" within the territory of my field of awareness. This being manifests certain structural features which must be evident for truth to be before (*prae*-esse) my field of consciousness. Jet me discuss each such feature.

The formal, namely structural properties of "the" truth *qua* being in my field are:

1. I initiate my investigation within my field of consciousness by attending to or focusing my attention upon an object, be it a specific concrete thing (such as visible faces) or abstract ideas. I claim to be seeing faces, seats, an auditorium, etc. I hereby intentionally select a specific object which I intend to understand, comprehend, know or simply judge as being of such and such an intelligible nature. From a logical point of view one can say that the object of judgment is the "logical object", relative to which truth is to be predicated.

2. In order cognitively to approach the logical object selected, it is necessary to capture or (to speak in Whiteheadian terms) to prehend in apprehension the logical object, at least to a degree, in its intelligibility. The vectorial directionality of the act of intellection leads me to conceptualize the object not yet fully understood. A conceptualization, once ascertained, presents me with an intelligible structure, namely, a concept which I then use in order to understand the logical object and to assert truly cognitive judgments about it. Take the above conceptualization of a face as an example.

3. By means of conceptualization I can affect a comparison of the logical object with the developed conceptualization. I thereby relate the conceptualization with its intended object and determine the conformity of one moment with the other. The act that realizes this comparison is precisely the act of judging which in positive cases results in a declaration that the conformity "is true" or "'the truth is that the judgment has correctly judged the judgeable as it is." In other words, the judgment corresponds to or conforms with the logical object in its very intelligibility.

4. The three features that I have just enumerated are inexorable features present to the consciousness that is judging. The features are not, however, sufficient to generate "the" being of truth in my consciousness. They are without doubt a *sine qua non*, that is, they are before my field of consciousness whenever I judge about the truth of a proposition. But there is one more essential characteristic that generates "the" very being of truth before my field of consciousness. This generative act entails the recognition or acknowledgement of and assent to the conformity or correspondence so understood and appropriated by my intellection. In other words, I appropriate for my conscious self the logical object truly judged as it is, that is, I convert the judgment into my insight and hence into *my* truth. Truth thereby enters into my field of consciousness being present before me. It is precisely the prehension, apprehension, recognition, acknowledgment, and assenting that enables truth *to be* in my field of of consciousness, and thereby constitutes "the" very being of truth. I summarize the discussion asserting: The very being of truth in my field of consciousness is made present by the conscious act of judging the intelligible object of and from itself being before me, myself too being of and from myself. The act of judging itself entails necessarily recognizing, acknowledging and assenting to the conformity, namely, correspondence grasped by my intellection. My consciousness thereby appropriates "the" truth as it is before my field of consciousness. And it is such an appropriation, that makes "being present", is exactly the very being of "the" truth in my consciousness. It thereby becomes clear that "the" being of truth shares identity with the very being of my cognizing consciousness, or truth simply is not. This definitional thesis has momentous consequences.

If the conscious act of appropriation is excluded from a concept of truth, truth simply disappears because it has lost its "being" in "the" being of my field of consciousness. There is no truth unless it possesses being before the being of my consciousness! The mere agreement of propositions with the logical object results in absolutely no truth whatsoever. To be sure, this relation must be determined, but it does not constitute truth in its being, or more precisely, the very being of truth. This means that limiting the examination of truth to a propositional relation has misled much reflection on truth in the twentieth century. The relation is, certainly, a necessary feature of truth, although it lacks the sufficiently structural factor that enables truth to be, namely consciousness intentionally being aware of it. Truth-being is identical with "the" field-being of my judging consciousness. Without my prehending, apprehending, judging, recognizing, acknowledging, and assenting, there is no truth in my solipsistically postulated world and, as will be shown, in no world of any kind whatsoever. I am getting ahead of myself here. So back to "the" being of truth my field of awareness in the form of a final summation.

I shall dare a sort of ontological formulation concerning the being of truth in and only in the field of consciousness of my solipsistic postulated world. The ontological thesis that I will present is valid at this point only for anything being before my field of consciousness. In order to explain myself I will make use of a philosophical proposal by Robert Reininger. I must note that Reininger in no way restricted his thesis to a limited field. His thesis was understood by him to be valid universally for reality *per se*, that is, without any field limitations. I, however, will provisionally limit Reininget's thesis solely to my field of consciousness suggesting merely a field-ontology. I will cite very selectively and partially from a key section of Reininger's *magnum opus* and apply his thesis to the solipsistic world methodologically postulated by myself. My postulated *solipsism* possesses its own ontology! Later in this study I shall extend Reininger's idealism to reality *per se*. This extension will take place when I take up the problem of *the* being of truth *per se*. But now to Reininger's words which will not be commented upon for the moment. "There is for us no being that would be outside conscious being [*bewusstes Sein*]. It immediately follows that no affirmation about the absolutely non-conscious [*das schlechthin Unbewusste*] would be possible... . Consciousness [*Bewusstheit*] ... is the indispensable feature, the *character indelibilis*, of everything which can be the-object of our reflections.[16]

VI. Problematization of the Previous Argument

There is a weakness in my argumentation derived from my methodological *solipsism* itself. In other words, in order to realize a judgment of truth I have to be able to compare consciously the conceptualization with the logical object in order to be able to have cognitive awareness of the correspondence, conformity, or coincidence in all adequacy with the logical object which presents itself in my field of consciousness. Moreover, there is no possibility of accurately effecting such a judgment if the object itself has not been fully or, worse, cannot be captured, namely, (ap)prehended by my intellective consciousness while rendering judgment. Doubts concerning the capture as a possibility constitute exactly the problematic which could render my argument, including truth itself, illusions of a solipsist, one all too theoretically confused in his philosophical *hubris*. (I think Rorty would agree.)

Let me consider my brief definition of the human face. Sometime back while walking through the streets of a large city in Germany I saw in a shop window what appeared to be the face of a person. Suddenly my vision blurred and this face turned partially into a type of chaotic manifoldness such that I seemed to be seeing at the very same time both a face of flesh and a plastic face of a model dummy. This undecided vision indicated two distinct things, yet without sufficient individualization in order to resolve the apparent contradiction. What was it that I had apprehended being of and from itself? My judgment vacillated and oscillated leaving me in cognitive perplexity. Upon approaching the window and while staring attentively at the ambivalent "thing," suddenly a clarification took place resulting in the capture of a single object whose conceptualization coincided with the intelligibility that justifies the assertion that the truth is that the seen object is in reality just a plastic face. Did I just resolve all cognitive difficulties? No! In each specific act of capturing something I cannot capture accurately (Rorty) that thing in one hundred percent of its all-encompassing totality because I can continue on temporally without ending the process of (ap)prehending the object from ever more points of view. Who knows? Maybe a closer examination of the plastic face tomorrow will reveal it to be of flesh and blood. I seem to have just formulated a very grave problematic. And I have!

This illustration might appear trivial, but it is not. On the contrary, it points to a fundamental problematic which constitutes the errant pathway of many reflections about the sciences, evident in the battle between realism and anti-realism, not to speak of philosophy up to Rorty and beyond. Rorty himself has rejected whatever pretension on the part of human reason to ground the comparison between the conceptualization and the real world leaving philosophy as an object of demystification, as an illusion. If Rorty is correct, the being of truth of my field of consciousness cannot, and on principle, extend beyond its own boundaries and, as I have just shown, it does not even seem to be able to suffice for this field itself.

In short, following Rorty, the ensuing is impossible: "To know is to represent accurately what is outside the mind; so, to understand the possibility and nature of knowledge is to understand the way in which the mind is able to construct such representations."[17] It would seem that the impossibility "to construct such representations" has just been shown! Consequently, knowledge grasped as truth apparently cannot be established because I, even in my methodological *solipsism*, cannot fully capture the logical object about which I wish to predicate merely "the" truth, not to speak of the world beyond my field. Without being able to capture fully the logical object, I cannot realize an "accurate," namely, "adequate" comparison of my conceptualization with the never fully prehended object. I can collect samples upon samples, apparently "verifying" my conceptualization. However, I can never exhaust all possible samples. Alas, this immediately raises the problem of verity entailed in induction about which Whitehead has written: "We want to conclude that the abstract conditions, which hold for the samples, also hold for all other entities which, for some reason or other, appear to be of the same sort. This process of reasoning from the sample to the whole species is induction. The theory of induction is the despair of philosophy - and yet all our activities are based upon it."[18] Induction is particularly the despair of a philosophy of knowledge. Within the terms of my description of my field of consciousness, this "despair" is grounded in the impossibility of realizing a fully adequate comparison such that I can never know just how accurate the sampling has been. It would seem that Rorty has won the argument and that my dreams about obtaining truth are nothing but the philosophical phantasies of my "mind." There is certainly something of importance to reflect on here!

If Rorty is correct that my (or anyone's) theory of correspondence is not valid for anything beyond the "mind" or, in the framework of my argumentation, beyond my field of consciousness, a question inexorably forces itself upon me. Rorty's thesis is not a mere product of induction, rather a universal *a priori* statement about the way things are outside his mind, even if this "way" means that we know that we cannot know anything "accurately," if at all. Rorty has not piled samples upon samples from which he, through a method of induction, concludes to the whole species, rather he has established *a priori* to any sampling that the "'species" in and of itself is unknowable and, hence, it is not possible to assert truth about it. Rorty's reasoning clearly refers to the way things are beyond his field of consciousness or, better, beyond "the mind" *per se*. Unwittingly, Rorty has clearly asserted that truth is that things are such that truth simply is not possible. It is true that Rorty is, at least, implicitly claiming that his conceptualization of the problem corresponds to the nature of the situation and said situation refers to the entirety of the "outside." And such a claim, be it but implicit, is a truth assertion that goes beyond his "mind" or, in my terms, his field of consciousness! This is, indeed, an *aporia*! More importantly, this *aporia* offers me a way to transcend "the" truth in my field of consciousness and approach the truth per se, that is, without limitations to a field (or to a "'mind").

VII. The Being of Truth as Such

An *aporia* is a rational difficulty which apparently has no solution. A solution is only possible if the part of the argumentation that leads to the *aporia* can be found-and clarified. I contend that the difficulties in Rorty's work resides in the failure to distinguish between truth in its formality and truth in its materiality. The objections offered touch on truth only in its materiality which is never fully attainable. But, as is evident in the cases of Devitt, Sommers, and Rorty himself, all quoted in the first paragraph of this investigation (though I could easily tender a dozen or more theorists), there is absolutely no awareness of the distinction between formality and materiality relative to truth. The truth is: those who deny correspondence truth do so by formulating propositions and applying them in accordance with the paradigmatic pattern of correspondence, conformity or coincidence! The difficulty producing the *aporia* thereby remains hidden from rational reflection as it is terminologically blurred, namely, linguistically liquidated. My discussion of "the" being of truth as such finds its starting point in the disjunction between materiality and formality.

I must first examine the *aporia* entailed. Rorty has repeatedly proclaimed that "truth" has no reference to anything "outside the mind," his and mine (leaving it unclear if it has any application to anything inside his mind which would include his very statement). This is rampant dogmatism, all wrapped up in a statement evincing the structure of correspondence. In short, Rorty has *de facto* pronounced a truth that his principles do not permit as ontologically pronounceable. If it is truly so that there is no application of correspondence assertions to what is "outside the mind,' then such a correspondence affirmation simply nullifies itself. Rorty has uttered an assertion, the conceptual content of which conforms with or corresponds to the real nature of things in the "outside." Indeed, any assertion about an "outside the mind," be it positive, negative or agnostic, necessarily pretends to represent the nature of "outside the mind" as the realm really is, particularly relevant to the judging thinker, no matter how skeptical he might think he is.

I hereby return to my description of how I generate, conceive and realize truth in my field of consciousness. Specifically, "the" truth in my field receives its being through and in the reflective judgment directed toward the conformity of my conceptualization with the logical object, intentionally referred to by myself as a truth-seeking subject. Within the confines of my field I have described the objective and subjective aspects of this field leading to the four necessary essentials that must be in order for truth, being in and from itself, to be present before me, being of and from myself. It was also noted initially that such a methodological *solipsism* is not self-sustaining. The mere fact that I distinguish my field from any possible other field or from a totality outside the range of my consciousness means that I am already directing my judging toward that "outside." Otherwise, my methodological *solipsism* has no meaning. My exclusion of such reality entails implicitly a truth claim, namely that such an exclusion is methodologically valid. If my strategy is valid, and I do assert this, then I have surreptitiously predicated something about that which is beyond the range of my intentionally directed awareness. I tried to hold myself in my discussion to the "inside" of the range of my consciousness and discovered that even there I was forced to be reflective and critically evaluative of my descriptions, for example of the various types of faces I thought I had seen. To the degree that the logical object is apparently not what is appears to me to be, to that degree its being implies more than being only situated in the immediacy of my field of consciousness. After all, I had seen no Martian face and I was in error in seeing the ambiguous face of plastic vs flesh. I continually make revisions of my judgments that consequently refer to more than what is at any given instant present in my field. A *solipsism*, be it but methodological, is not encompassing enough for the very judgments of material truth that I do actually assert while remaining just in my field of awareness. I continually proclaim truth about things beyond my immediately present field of consciousness. How am I to come to terms with this possible *aporia* in my own method of analysis?

In establishing my theses on the four essentials necessarily present to me for there to be truth in and before my field of consciousness, I have shown that the conscious subject is structurally entailed in the very being of truth. In other words, when I qualify a judgment with the assertion: "It is true that... ," I have consciously focused upon a specific logical object, conceptualized said object, realized a judgment concerning a comparison between the conceptualization and the logical object, ascertained the correspondence, conformity or coincidence of the two factors and then reflected about the comparison such that I conscientiously recognize, acknowledge and assent to the conclusion that the comparison so judged is truly representative of that object. Without the essential feature of conscientiously acknowledging the consciously realized insight into the coincidence revealed in the comparison, truth (claims) do not have any being whatsoever and consequently are simply not. This determination of the features of "the" being of truth has, alas, led to an *aporia*-producing difficulty.

Should the prehension of the object not allow for an all-encompassing apprehension of the factors of comparison, any truth materially asserted lacks adequacy.[19] The structural inability of finite consciousness to apprehend the logical object fully and exhaustively renders truth in materiality as necessarily subject to doubt. Rorty's "outside" seems, indeed, to frustrate any possible truth claims. On the other hand, if any philosopher attempts to assert that whatever is "outside of the mind" is cognitively doubtful or even unknowable, that philosopher is, whether he or she wants to or not, asserting a "truth," indeed, a truth not limited to any specific kind of object, rather one that announces something formal of infinite extension, that is, valid universally for any possible material truth. And this means that the philosopher is pronouncing truth about that which he does not in any way prehend and, hence, with which he cannot compare directly his conceptualization. Paradoxically, Rorty's material claim that "it is not possible to specify the nature of truth" is in reality a truth in formality, that is, one that proclaims a structural formality valid for all material claims of truth. Leaving aside the theoretical oxymoron contained in Rorty's blatant specification of the "nature of truth", he has effectively claimed truth about the formal structure of whatever is "inside" and "outside the mind," that is, about what is. But Rorty admittedly possesses no direct awareness of that "outside the mind" *qua* being beyond awareness. It follows that the indispensable comparison that warrants the supposed validity of his truth (conveniently not mentioned as truth) is simply lacking. In reality, Rorty's statement is a pseudo-statement, since he has nothing in his "mind," namely consciousness, to which he can refer his conceptualization as the logical object to be judged. Rorty appears to have proclaimed something semantically meaningful, but in reality he has said nothing, lacking anything to which he can refer. Rorty's blatant nonsense is, nevertheless, not without value because it brings to light that the measure of the possibility of truth is at the same time claiming truth. Rorty thereby avails himself of a correspondence truth claim, however much he contradicts himself and proves my point. His self-blinding truth in formality will offer me the opportunity to reflect upon "the" being of truth *per se*. My discussion will entail two fundamental steps.

Step 1: Concluding my presentation of the four essential features of "the" truth in consciousness, I provisionally adduced some ideas from Reininger in order, so to speak, to construct a "my-field idealism." Since I had postulated methodological *solipsism*, I was obliged to limit Reininger's idealism to "my field of consciousness" and to nothing "outside." This limitation must now be revoked. I will at this point discuss Reininger again, citing a bit more of his thesis. Reininger will enable me to transcend the boundaries of my quite finite field of consciousness so as to enter into the "outside" so scourged by Rorty's criticism. First, I want to recall the final sentence of the statement quoted above: "Consciousness (*Bewusstheit*) ...is ... the character *indelebilis* of all that can be the object of our reflections." I must confess that I have not translated accurately the technical term *Bewusstheit*, something not appropriate at an earlier point in my argumentation. An explanation of my dereliction will reveal how I propose to transcend my field of consciousness in order to consider "the" being of truth *per se*.

I have not found *Bewusstheit* in a German dictionary readily at my disposal. Nevertheless, following the rules of German grammar, it is possible to conclude that the primary meaning is "that which pertains to or entails consciousness." The "pertaining to consciousness" is fully congruent with the framework of my analysis of presentness. Indeed, *Bewusstheit* and being present are two sides of presentness. In other words, "that which concerns consciousness" is constitutive of the being as it is in itself in presentness. Following my interpretation, Reininger's thesis would read better in English as: Presentness (*Bewusstheit*) is the *character indelibilis* of anything which can be the object of our reflections. Or with a slight alteration: The being of any object of our reflections is presentness (*Bewusstheit*). This is true even if there is nothing but my field of consciousness. The very being of the truth *per se* entails structurally a type of idealism, be it for my field or for reality in itself. Being pertains to presentness just as does *Bewusstheit*, both as subject and object, and this also includes the very Being of *the* truth *per se*, not only just in the being of my field.

In order to amplify my analysis, I shall proffer the Reininger challenge to all who wish to exclude consciousness from being, Alas, it must be noted that there are some difficulties in translating bewusst as In *Bewusstsein* or *Bewusstheit*. This forces me to be a bit free with my translation in order to render the intended meaning into English. Back to Reininger and to the quotation already cited above. I will now cite other parts of the same paragraph. At this point I am in no way limiting my idealistic thesis just to my field of consciousness alone, rather I am attempting a general ontological truth. Reininger contends that there "is no being that is not also conscious being [*bewußtes Sein*], from which it follows that no statement about an absolutely non-conscious thing or being [*ein schlechthin Unbewusstes*] would be possible, not even in the recognition that is 'is'... . Not only is thinking conscious, but also the objects that it must judge must also be so." At this point Reininger utters his challenge:

> Let one attempt sometime to direct one's thinking toward an absolutely non-conscious thing [*ein schlechthin Nicht-Bewusstes*]! I can know not only nothing about something in any way pertaining to consciousness [*von einem in keiner Weise Bewußsten*], but I cannot even say that I know nothing about it. Pertaining to consciousness [*Bewusstheit*] is not a predicate which applies to somethings with which one has to do and not with others. It [Bewusstheit] is rather a feature which cannot be thought away, it is the character *indelibilis* of everything that can be an object of our reflections.

I find Reininger's "challenge" in the first sentence of this quoted passage. I ask my reader to take up the challenge. If the reader can refute it, I lose the theoretical battle. So, let each person select something, let us say, a mere spot of green. Next, let us repress or remove in the most radical manner possible all presentness, namely, all of that which pertains to consciousness (*Bewusstheit*). Such a suppression absences immediately any "it manifesting itself from... to..., that is, the being constitutive of presentness. *Bewusstheit* is essential to presentness and hence to any object presenting itself therein. What remains of the spot of green once the experiment of repression is rigorously realized? *"Ein schlechthin Unbewusstes"* becomes necessarily absolute non-presentness, absolute non-manifesting, in short, nothing, absolutely (schlechthin) at all. Boldly asserted, all objects that present themselves, once presentness is deleted, become simply nothing and nothing else, that is, a semantic nullity. There is yet more. The ubiquity of this nothingness is without limits such that the "of and from myself" – namely the "I," a co-structure of presentness-equally becomes nothing in the context postulated. Remove all that pertains to consciousness, namely *Bewusstheit*, and absolutely nothing remains, a nothing about which nothing is to be said because any sayer too is nothing, not to speak of the very "saying" itself. The world "outside the mind" of Rorty's scorn, as well as Rorty himself, become nothing; this is the woeful truth. In other words, any conceptualization, following Reininger's logic, when applied to a potential logical object can find absolutely nothing with which to conform or to which to correspond. And that is semantic absurdity. Every attempt to suggest an unknown if not unknowable "outside" *presentness per se* is pure nonsense, it is semantically vacuous. Glorious, but nonsense!

Step 2: An *aporia* is a difficulty of a rational nature that appears to permit no solution. For instance, in rejecting apodictically the preoccupation of philosophy with the attempt truly to represent reality as it is, Rorty effectively proffered a truth thesis that putatively is valid for everything "outside the mind"— mine as well as his. This constitutes an *aporia* without any possible solution within the terms of Rorty's own logic. Rorty has effectively proclaimed a correspondence truth that his very theoretical principles do not permit him ontologically to proclaim. If it is true that that there is no valid application of correspondence truth "outside the mind," then this very affirmation annuls itself transforms Rorty's assertion whether he like it or not into transcampal claims of correspondence. Rorty's aporia thereby becomes a contradiction, pure and simple! The philosophical situation is not so if we examine the idealistic implications contained in "the" very being of truth proper to my field of consciousness. I am now at the point of my analysis where it becomes necessary to transcend my self-imposed solipsism. I must consider the problematic of truth beyond the immediacy of and in my field of consciousness. What can Sommer's "objective relatum"[20] beyond my field of consciousness be? How am I to answer such staggering difficulties?

I find a suggestion for overcoming such an *aporia* in a book by Josiah Royce who, somewhat figuratively, writes: "The escape from the prison of the inner self [i.e., individual consciousness] is simply the fact that the inner self is through and through an appeal to a larger self ... that knows."[21] Interpreting my field of consciousness as a simile for "the inner self", the appeal proclaimed by Royce reveals itself to be a call for a larger conscious self whose size extends *ad infinitum*. What is this "larger self, "consciousness, whose immensity extends *ad infinitum*, and what is its relation to the smaller self of my field of consciousness? Just how can such an infinite Self overcome the *aporia* that Rorty has led us into? Just how does this infinitely larger self – indeed this "infinitely large Self"– make the truth formally possible?

I commenced my study with a specific tactic that has directed the argumentative use of "my field of consciousness," thereby excluding any beyond. This exclusion enabled me to delineate the ontological structure of "the" truth within the finite boundaries of my consciousness. If a truth assertion is to be made in said field, it is obvious that a judging "I" so ventures the claim. I sought to grant to my field of consciousness the ontological status of a regional "'field-idealism" using some concepts from the idealist Reininger. Following my methodology of *solipsism* I provisionally restricted the validity of his ontological claims to the range of my field of consciousness. At this point I hereby rescind such provisionality. I now intend to view the theses of Reininger as possessing (exactly as Reininger himself intended) unlimited application. Reininger's most essential point lies in the final sentence of the selection quoted above which I now translate more accurately as: "That which pertains to consciousness [*Bewusstheit*]... is... the character indelibilis of everything that can be the object, of our reflections." Included in "the objects of our reflections" is of course truth. If I am to explain the possibility, let alone assert the actuality of the truth as valid beyond my field of consciousness – that is, if my explanation is to proffer "truth" about truth – then I must structure my argumentation about the "outside the mind" such that what is predicated cannot be denied without a self-contradiction. A contradiction can indeed be captured, namely apprehended by my judging finite consciousness. That which cannot be denied as true, except at the price of contradiction, simply and purely is! Try as I might (and as Rorty has so mightily tried), truth assertions claiming validity for things beyond the limits of my "mind" (to use Rorty's terminology) are continually uttered by myself and, I believe, by others within the framework of each's own field of consciousness. If persons deny that there be any truth about things beyond their own awareness (or their "mind"), they have contradicted themselves with said agnosticism. In other words, if there is no correspondence truth, this too is a fact that corresponds to the way reality is *per se*, that is, beyond my or any finite consciousness. The truth entails of necessity being actually infinite! The inexorable question follows: being actually infinite before what type of consciousness *qua* its being? Such a consciousness must be all-encompassing in its endless circumspect comprehension. Correlatively, it must be transcampal or, to use proper terminology, transcendent of all finite fields of consciousness. Expressed differently; there must be an all-encompassing, infinite consciousness of the logical object or no truth whatsoever can be. At this point, Royce's appeal to "a larger self" as an "infinite Self" begins to reveal its decisive meaning. Since truth within and beyond any finite field, namely, any finite self, cannot be denied without said denial itself becoming an absolute truth, a problem, if not an *aporia*, immediately appears. The conclusion of my previous argument is that truth only is by being before a judging "I" or self. But my or any finite "I" (self) cannot capture or (ap)prehend the logical object in its endless entirety. Such a capture does, indeed, require an actually infinite Self that knows. Such a self is an all-encompassing consciousness before which all reality is in presentness (*Bewusstheit*). This necessity grounds "the" being of truth *per se*. Why?

We can understand why Royce expands "a larger self ... that knows" into an infinite Self conceived as knowing in absolutely infinite fullness. The correspondence pertaining between the subject's conceptualization and the conceptualized object ontologically necessitates an infinite comprehension. Royce's thesis cannot be denied without grounding the denial in absolute truth or falling into a self-contradiction. Referring to this all-encompassing knowing, Royce designates said knower as "God". Royce writes: "I propose to define ... 'God', by using what tradition would call one of the Divine Attributes, ... [i.e.] Omniscience. ... By the word 'God' I shall mean...a being who is conceived as possessing to the full all logically possible knowledge, insight, wisdom."[22] The "larger self" turns out to transcend all finite regions because it is infinite, absolute and, hence, omniscient. Without the being of omniscient consciousness, there is verily no truth whatsoever, including this very thesis itself. The Being of the truth and the Being of an omniscient knower coincide in identical Being. The "objective *relatum*" to which the truth refers is the logical object grasped by an infinitely "larger self ... that knows" omnisciently that *relatum*, thereby solving Sommer's problem. This omniscient Self was rightly designated by Royce as God. Before I briefly reflect upon the divine nature of this logically necessitated foundation of the truth I shall seek very briefly to connect absolute truth in formality with relative truths in materiality.

Truth evinces two aspects: materiality and formality. My declared truths continually diverge materially, often enough contradicting each other, never fully accurate, seemingly always open to revision; all of which reveals that there is error! This is so, I conclude, because I, as a finite possessor of truth, cannot in principle ever capture (prehend) the totality of any finite object, leaving me (and any finite mind for that matter) prisoner to the inexorable inadequacy of my correspondence truths relative to the richness of their materiality. In short, cognitive fallibility relative to the materiality of truth(s) is a function of the very structure of the human "self ... that knows," namely finitude.

If my argumentation has been correct, then the truth formally possesses features that are intrinsic to any material assertion claiming to be true. This means that the truth *per se* can well function in a manner similar to pure reason in Kant's philosophy, that is it can be regulatory of the form that any material truth will evince, whether or not such a truth can withstand examination, indeed, whether or not it is judged as truly being in error. A few words only will have to suffice for an understanding of the regulatory function.

Concerning this interpretative process, Bernard Bosanquet has written: "The process of construction [of judgments] is always that of exhibiting a whole in its parts, i.e., an identity in its differences. ... The objects of knowledge differ in the mode of relation between their parts and the whole, and thus give rise to different types of judgment and inference."[23] And just what is the importance of Bosanquet's thesis? The "objects of knowledge," be their claims of long duration of just passing opinion, will manifest in all truth assertions *qua* their materiality a formal congruence of a whole which seemingly establishes an identity in its differences. Knowledge formally consists of the relation between the manifold and the whole constituting a congruency of identity. New knowledge, which replaces former truths, will evince a new mode of relation between parts and whole. This relationality constitutes the regulatory form that new material truths will assume. The cosmology of Aristotle eventually surrendered to the cosmology of Newton, whose own paradigms are dissolving into theories of relativity and quanta, exactly as the human face in the store window changed into the plastic face that it was all along. Whatever the new aspirant to truth in materiality will be, it will evince the very formality described by Bosanquet. In this way, it becomes evident that truth in formality offers a regulatory norm for whatever truths in materiality will seem most plausible, most probable. In fact, there are many kinds of epistemological theories seeking some formal criteria for material truth, e.g., coherence, corroboration, convergence, intersubjective consensus and, even in a way, pragmatism. This list is not meant to be exhaustive. With my brief discussion of truth in materiality now concluded, I return to Royce's designation of the "larger self" as God.

VII. Conclusion

In order to ascertain the very possibility of truth (as he also had done for error), Royce solved the problem of the inadequacy of (ap)prehension by arriving at an absolutely infinite Self who grasps exhaustively the entire plethora of logical objects in their endless features, variations, aspects, etc. This Self is God. Just what is the ontological relation between God and the truth? Royce does not systematically develop an answer here. For a more strictly theological understanding I will leave Royce and migrate to St. Anselm of Canterbury (1033-1109). Anselm was certainly the first of the great medieval philosopher-theologians and, perhaps to this day, has evolved the most comprehensive philo-theological interpretation of God as being truth. Particularly inspiring for my reflections is Anselm's *De Veritate* (1082-85), along with his *Proslogion* (1077)[24]. However, before proceeding I should note that my Roycean idealism is conceptually foreign to Anselm. This means, of course, that I will be interpreting Anselm through Roycean categories, that is, only reflecting in an Anselmian manner.

Anselm begins his treatise on truth with the question: "Because we believe that *God is truth* and because we say that truth is in many other things, I wish to know whether, whenever truth is spoken of, we ought to be saying the truth is in all things?"' (Cap. I). I have placed "God is truth" in italics in order to highlight the radicalness implied by an omniscient God, that is, in terms of God's formal linkage with truth materially asserted about all things, which is to say "'in all things." Viewed in Anselmian terms: God is Truth! This thesis is comprehensible within the terms of my idealistic analysis of the Being (*esse*) of truth as realized above. In other words, I have in effect resolved Anselm's query by showing that, in Anselm's words, truths in all things receive their ultimate justification as truth being (before) God. Let me sketch out my adoption of Anselm's reflections on the "being" of God Who is Truth.

Above I described how "the" truth acquires being present in, or better, before my field of consciousness. I sought to establish that both the being of the object known *qua* truth and the being of the knowing subject qua truth judgment coincide in the selfsame identity of the very-Being of consciousness (*Bewusstheit*). There are not two beings relative to which some connective bridge is to be sought. The identity of shared Being resolves the apparent problematic. However, once this identity is torn asunder, the two shall never again meet as the history of modern thought has repeatedly demonstrated. I find Rorty's blanket denial of truth to be a welcome dogmatic stance because he simply and logically rejects any connection between any objectivity to which the human knower might truly correspond. It has been the aim of my study to respond to Rorty's thesis.

The dynamics of my reply commenced with the nature of truth in my field of consciousness, *solipsisticly* postulated. However, I soon discovered that, within my *solipsism*, my ability, simply due to my finitude, prevents me from ever grasping adequately and accurately any logical object intended for a judgment of correspondence truth. The *relatum* in its totality remains beyond my prehensive capacity and threatens me with the very strictures proposed by Rorty. Such considerations led me to the insight that "the" truth in my field of consciousness is not self-sufficient, rather leads to a transcampal realm which is logically necessary or no statements whatsoever, even of skepticism, are possible since they refer literally to nothing. Here Reininger's idealistic identification of being (*esse*) and *Bewusstheit* entered the argument. Following Reiningerian logic, I affirmed an all-knowing Self-(consciousness) relative to Whom all candidates for being logical objects have their presentness, that is, are by being before consciousness. There is no being of anything unless its being made present achieves *Bewusstheit*. With this insight, I came to the conclusion of an infinite Self and accepted Royce's designation of that reality as God.

God, before whom all truth is present, makes present with absolute adequacy the endless manifold of the universe and thereby transforms divine awareness of this universe into the truth thereabout. The very being of the truth *qua* known coincides in identity with the being of an infinite God *qua* knowing. Following Anselm, I assert the following: God is Truth! And the reason? The truth is only insofar as it has presentness being before infinite consciousness and infinite consciousness *qua* knowing has being only by making present the truth. This shared Being justifies in my idealistic judgment the Anselmian thesis that God is Truth.

My analysis would end in an idealistic pantheism if I were to claim that the sole knowing realized by God is that of the universe in its manifold of endless finitude.[25] I reject any such circumscription of divine consciousness! My denial derives from the nature of the very actual infinity constitutive of divine Being, an infinity which in and of itself excludes all finitude. Heterogeneity reigns between finitude and actual infinitude. I have discussed this problematic in a previous study in a journal.[26] Divine reality entails Being infinitely (*esse infinite*) and, hence, is not exhausted by awareness (*Bewusstheit*) of the world. Consequently, when we begin to reflect upon God's own Self-consciousness, we enter into an area of theology of extreme difficulty, namely how to predicate anything to transcendent divinity *qua* it being infinitely transcendent.[27] Any discussion of divine Self-awareness is beyond the scope of my reflections which have been restricted solely to the problem of (the) truth relative to the universe in which we humans seek to assert some truth. I will venture no further speculations here. Instead I will allow Anselm to conclude my current ruminations, hopefully inspiring readers to meditate for themselves upon the suggestive thoughts of a truly profound theologian. I cite from Anselm's *Proslogion*:

> Nothing contains You and You contain all things (Cap. XIX).
> You alone penetrate and embrace all things. You are prior and beyond all things (Cap. XX).

You are Who, most properly and simply, has neither past nor future being, rather only being present (Cap. XIII).

You, Lord, are singularly uncircumspect [infinite] and eternal (Cap.XIII).

Therefore, Lord, not only are you that of which nothing greater can be thought, rather something greater than can be thought (Cap. XV).

If one does not see You, one sees neither light nor truth (Cap. XIV).

Speak now, my whole heart says unto to God: "I seek Your countenance, I desire Your countenance" (Cap. I).

I do not seek to understand in order to believe, rather I believe in order to understand (Cap. I).

Footnotes

1   Michael Devitt, *Realism and Truth* (Princeton: Princeton University Press, 1991), 35, 37.

2   Fred Sommers, "Existence and Correspondence-to-fact," in *Formal Ontology*, ed. Roberto Pol and Peter Simon (Dordrecht: Kluwer Academic Publishers, 1996), 135.

3   Richard Rorty, *Philosophical Papers*, vol. 3, *Truth and Progress*, (Cambridge: Cambridge University Press, 1998), 3.

4   Richard Rorty, *Philosophy and the Mirror of Nature*, Princeton: Princeton University Press, 1980), 3.

5   Josiah Royce, *The Religious Aspect of Philosophy*: *A Critique of the Bases of Conduct* ? and of Faith (New York: Harper Torchbooks, 1958), 384-435.

6   Alain Lercher, *Les mots de la philosophie* (Paris: Belin, 1985), 90-91.

7   The potentiality of *solipsism* in realistic terms is made evident in Brand Blanshard's highly destructive critique of logical positivism beginning with a deconstruction of Wittgenstein. Cf. Blanshard, *Reason and Analysis* (La Salle: Open Court, 1964). In the context of his critique of Wittgenstein, Blanshard shows with sparkling clarity that Wittgenstein did *de facto concoct a "Solipsism* Without a Subject,' cf. 197-205.

8   Robert Reininger, *Metaphysik der Wirklichkeit*, 2nd ed., (München: Ernst Reinhardt Verlag, 1970), 11-12.

9   The technical term "field of consciousness" is taken from the Aron Gurwitch. *La theorie du champ de la conscience* (Desclée: Neuve Brouwer, 1957).

10 The specific form of correspondence theory that I have found most influential is that of Mariano Alvarez Gomez, "Sobre el concepto de verdad," in *Pensamiento del ser y espera de Dios* (Salamanca: Sígueme, 2004), 437-77. I differ from Prof. Alvarez in that I integrate Royce' idealist theory with the notion of correspondence: this integration wall become evident in the evolution of the following argument in the text.

11 Gerhard Huber, *Eidos und Existenz: Umrisse einer Philosophie der Gegenwärtigkeit* (Basel: Schwabe & Co. AG, 1995), 17-39,

12 Huber explains his use of *"Gegenwärtigkeit"* in the following words: "Das Etymon in 'wärts' bedeutet ein mit 'werden' verwandtes 'sich wenden' (lateinisch 'vertere'). *'Gegenwärtig' ist also das, was im Gegen und Gegenüber einem zuwendet. Gegenwärtigkeit ist Da-sein als Zugewendetsein. Welt und Dinge in*

ihr sind gegenwärtig als mir zugewendet.' 21. The various German terms used all evince the directionality entailed in the Latin verb as can be seen in any German dictionary for Latin. In short, the root meaning is a "turning/turned towards." This directionality will be a determinant of the ensuing analysis.

13 I have purposely used the term "presentness" in order to avoid any necessity of relating the notion to time. Craig Bourne has argued that only the "present" exists. This "fact" is the source of his philosophy of "presentism." Cf. Bourne, *A Future for Presentism* (Oxford: Clarendon Press, 2006). Bourne seeks to show how "presentism" is related to the tenses of past and future. In my discussion, I am only interested in the fact that whatever enters my field of consciousness is "present," that is, it is before my consciousness. Accordingly, I treat being "present" atemporally.

14 Alfred North Whitehead, *Science and the Modern World* (New York: A Mentor Book, 1948), 63. 67, and 135. Whitehead writes: "I will use the word prehension for non-cognitive apprehension: by this I mean apprehension which may or may not be cognitive," (67).

15 My conceptualization of intelligibility is derived from interweaving the reflections of two thinkers, namely: Manfred Zahn, "Einheit" in Handbuch philosophischer Grundbegniffe, eds. Herman Krings, Hans Michael Baumgarten, and Christoph Wild (München: Kosel Verlag, 1973), 2:321-27 and specially Bernard Bosanquet, *The Essentials of Logic Being Ten Lectures on Judgment and Inference* (London: Macmillan & Co, 1960), 54-59. Bosanquet was perhaps the leading English idealist of his time.

16 Reininger, *Metaphysik der Wirklichkeit*, 24.

17 Rorty, *Philosophy and the Mirror of Nature*, 3. 3

18 Whitehead, *Science and the Modern World*, 29.

19 Long before Rorty's criticism Xavier Zubiri has perceptively pointed out the often overlooked distinction between conformity and adequacy. A thesis can conform with its object without adequately describing it. Cf. Zubin, *El problema filosofico de la historia de las religiones* (Madrid: Alianza, 1993), 153-55.

20 There is no truth without a logical object in some way "external" to the asserting consciousness. This fact has burdened much philosophy since the Logical Positivists on to Rorty. A brilliant, but structurally doomed attempt can be found in Michael Bergman's daring "justification" of the validity of "epistemic externalism" in his *Justification Without Awareness: A Defense of Epistemic Externalism* (Oxford: Clarendon Press, 2006). Desperate attempts to justify an

externality for the logical object led, I suspect, Rorty plausibly to reject correspondence truth as a possibility.

21 Cf. Royce, *The Spirit of Modern Philosophy* (Boston: Houghton, 1892}, 374.

22.Cf. Royce, *The Conception of God* (New York: MacMillan., 1897), 7.

23 Cf. Bosanquet, *The Essential of Logic*, 57-58.

24 Cf. Anselm of Canterbury, *Über die Wahrheit. Lateinisch-Deutsch*, ed. Marcus
   Enders (Limburg: Meiner Verlag, 2001) and Anselmo, *Proslogion*, ed. Miguel
   Pérez de Laborda (Pamplona, ENUSA, 2002). Translations into English will be
   mine and references will be indicated by the relevant capitulum.

25 Merging divine consciousness with awareness of the world alone has led the
   idealist T. I. S. Sprigge to transform Roycean idealism into a "pantheistic idealism" in his magisterial *The God of Metaphysics* (Oxford: Clarendon Press,
   2008), 473-533.

26 Leonard P. Wessell, "Definitions of Infinity: An Attempt to Gain Conceptual
   Clarity with Mathematical and Theological Ramifications, *Sino-Christian Studies*, no. 12 (2011):67 - 103.

27 Just to illustrate the often tedious care medieval theologians took to justify
   talk about God in Godself, cf. St. Thomas Aquinas's *Sancti Thomae Aquinalis
   Compendium Theologiae* (1261), ed. Friedrich Albert (Wurzburg. Andreas
   Göbel's Verlag, 1896). Thomas dedicates the first 36 sections of the entire 236
   to grounding metaphysically the nature of the divine Self before beginning his
   theological examination of revelation from God.

Bibliography

Álvarez Gómez, Mariano. *Pensamiento del ser y espera de Dios*. Salamanca: Sígueme, 2004.

Anselm, Saint. *De Veritate* (1082-1085). Reprinted in *Über die Wahrheit*. Lateinisch-Deutsch. Edited by Marcus Enders. Hamburg: Meiners Verlag, 2001.

_____. *Proslogion*. Reprinted in *Prosolgion*. Edited by Miguel Pérez de Laborda. Pamplona: UNUSA, 2002.

Aquinas, Thomas. *Sancti Thomae Aquinatatis COMPENDIUM THEOLOGIAE*. Edited by Friedrich Albert. Würzberg: Andreas Göbel's Verlag, 1896.

Bergman, Michael. *Justification Without Awareness. A Defense of Epistemic Externalism*. Oxford: Claredon Press, 2006.

Blanshard, Brand. *Reason and Analysis*. La Salle Open Court, 1964.

Devitt, Michael. *Realism and Truth*. Princeton: Princeton University Press, 1991.

Gurwitch, Aron. *La théorie du champ de la conscience*. Declée: DeBouwer, 1957.

Huber, Gerhard. *Eidos und Existenz: Umrisse einer Philosophie der Gegenwärtigkeit*. Basel: Schwabe & Co, 1995.

Lecher, Alain. *Les mots de la philosophie*. Paris: Berlin, 1985.

Reininger, Robert. *Metaphysik der Wirklichkeit*. 2 Vols. München: Ernst Reinhardt Verlag, 1970.

Rorty, Richard. *Philosophy and the Mirror of Nature*. Princeton: Princeton University Press, 1998.

_____. Vol. 3, *Truth and Progress*. Cambridge: Cambridge University Press, 1998.

Royce, Josiah. *The Religious Aspect of Philosophy: A Critique of the Bases of Conduct and Faith*. Houghton, Miffin & Co, 1885. Reprint, New York Harper Torchbooks, 1958.

_____. *The Spirit of Modern Philosophy*. Boston: Houghton, 1892. Sommers Fred. "Existence and Correspondence-to-fact." In *Formal Ontology*. Edited by Roberto Poli and Peter Simon. Dordrecht: Kluwer Academic Publishers, 1996. Pp. 131-59.

Sprigge, T. L. S. *The God of Metaphysics*. Oxford: Claredon Press, 2008.

Wessell, Leonard P. "Definitions of Infinity: An Attempt to Gain Conceptual Clarity with mathematical and Theological Ramifications," in *Journal of Sino-Christian Studies*. No. 12 (2011): 67-103.

Zahn, Manfred. "Einheit," in *Handbuch philosophischer Begriffe*, Band 2. Edited by Herman Krings, Michael Baumgarten, und Christoph Wild. München: Kösel Verlag, 1973. Pp. 321-27.

Zubiri, Xavier. *El problema filosófico de la historia de las religiones*. Madrid: Alanza, 1993.

Chapter 3

Definitions of Infinity:

Abstract

At least since the time of Aristotle a distinction has been made between potential and actual infinity. Before the work of Georg Cantor, actual infinity was generally limited to being an ontological category most appropriate for a discussion of divinity. Infinity was generally absent from mathematical considerations. With Cantor the attempt was made to conceive of a series of natural numbers, potentially infinite because of its endlessness, as a totality or whole. Such a consideration renders actual infinity accessible to mathematical theorizing. Whereas medieval philosophers allowed for only one actual exemplification of infinity, suddenly there was a plethora, indeed, an infinity of infinite numbers. My intention in the following discussion is to achieve conceptual clarity so as to be able to render a rational judgment concerning the totalization of a series potentially without end, i.e., its transformation into actual infinity conceived of as an infinite number or as God qua infinity: This is achieved by producing definitions of potential and actual infinity as a preface to the formulation of a judgment on the logical integrity of actual infinities in mathematics and theology. This method follows leads to a fundamental critique of previous conceptualizations of infinity for mathematical and theological use and finds actual infinity to be a conceptual oxymoron when applied to mathematics and problematic when applied to theology.

Key-words: potential infinity, actual infinity, negative theology, positive theology, exclusionary method

According to Richard Rorty, philosophy in its essence does not pursue metaphysical truth, but rather seeks improved forms of linguistic communication and understanding between speakers. Indeed, philosophy is akin to literature, a type of literary criticism. Be that as it may, as an educated, long-time student of both literature as well as philosophy, I find something quite literarily dramatic in the philosophical "story" of infinity, in its metaphysical, mathematical and theological dimensions. This "tale" has recently been narrated in some 600+ pages by Manuel Cabada Castro[1], who commences with the ancient Greeks and pursues the mathematical history of infinity up to its revolutionary rethinking in the nineteenth century, particularly in the mathematics of Georg Cantor. It is at just this point that Cabada's "narration", if considered as a literary work, generates my consternation. How is the "hero," infinity, to be grasped conceptually? A significant dramatic tension in Cabada's history of infinity reveals essential changes in the interpretation of infinity, particularly in its potential and actual dimensions. Though trained in philosophy, I lack extensive formation in mathematics. On the contrary, I belong to the camp of "metaphysicians" who relegate infinity, in the context of the finite realm, to potentiality, whereas *"infinitum actu"* is attributed entitatively to divine reality. In order to understand the dilemma, I have initiated the ensuing study as an attempt to grasp conceptually the nature of "potential" and "actual" infinity and, hopefully, to render a rational judgment on its mathematical and theological ramifications. I will offer definitions of potential and actual infinity, followed by a limited commentary on the rational relevance of actual infinity for mathematics and theology. But first, let me explain my deepening perplexity.

I. Introduction to the Problem

The main character of Cabada's philosophical narrative, namely infinity, takes on oppositional features that would render any hero suspect in a literary narrative. Infinity is explicitly the "hero" of Cabada's historical "novel" and this hero, if it were really a living person, would seem to develop multiple personalities, i.e., losing its unicity *qua* actuality in order to become an infinite number of numerical actualities. The story being narrated here can be placed in focus by briefly contrasting Cantor's thought with some reflections on infinity by a leading Spanish Thomist, namely Antonio Millán-Puelles. In his philosophical lexicon, Millán-Puelles treats infinity as the primary entitative attribute of God[2]. From this attribute, Millán-Puelles then derives the utter simplicity and absolute unicity of God *qua* being infinite. Millán-Puelles, as with his medieval predecessors, is fully aware of the distinction between potential and actual infinity. In no way does Millán-Puelles reject the medieval thesis *"Infinitum actu non datur,"* i.e., insofar as such a formulation refers to the realm of finitude. In other words, actual infinity has no evident application to the numerical in mathematics. In Millán-Puelles' discussion of infinity as an actual entitative attribute, mathematical infinity is quite irrelevant because *"infinitum actu"* or *"infinitum in actu"* (both formulations can be found in the theology of Thomas Aquinas) is conceived of as referring to divine reality, not to mathematical quantity. Within finitude no actual infinity, not to speak of actual infinities, is given nor, indeed, even conceivable. Millán-Puelles uses the uniqueness of actual infinity as the basis for grounding divine simplicity and unicity. There is no plurality of actual infinities as such because (actual) infinity cannot be conceptualized in the terms of multiplicity. If it could be, polytheism may become rational possibility. According to Millán-Puelles, divine reality is one.

Millán-Puelles' limitation of actual infinity to the status of unicity stands in radical opposition to Cantor's reflections. According to Cantor an endless series, e.g., natural numbers, can be thought of as all the elements of a numerical series being actually together in a numerical set. In other words, Cantor conceived of integers together as a completed whole ("Ding für sich") which constitutes an infinite magnitude, namely an infinite number. The set of such a consummated togetherness forms in actuality a completed totality, wherein all numbers in their entirety *qua* being elements are set together such that the set has an infinite number of members or, in the case of natural numbers, of positive integers. The endless series of 1, 2, 3, ... is totalized symbolically as {1, 2, 3, ...}. Cantor's introduction of actual infinity leads me into perplexities that are mathematically as confusing as if a historical novel told how Lenin was inspired in a dream by the Holy Virgin to return to Russia. Let me touch briefly on one logical difficulty.

"Logic" teaches us that the whole is greater than any of its parts. This thesis almost seems to be a tautology. But in Cantorian mathematics such logical certainty is not true. The set of all the integers of natural numbers possesses the same number of numerical elements as the subset of even numbers. This seeming contradiction to logic is achieved by pairing off *ad infinitum* the serialized members of the full numerical set with part of the entity of that set. Consequently, the actual infinity of natural numbers, i.e., {1, 2, 3, ...} is numerically equivalent to the subset of {2, 4, 6, ...}. In actual infinity, whole and part evince a numerical equivalence. Lilian R. Lieber, in her pedagogically excellent explanation of infinity, frankly states that the logic of finite sets and the logic of infinite sets, while respecting the ideal of non-contradiction, can vary in logical rules, as exemplified in the equivalence of whole and part just given[3]. What holds for finite logic does not hold for the logic of infinity. In a one-to-one equivalence of actual infinities, the totality of numerical members of all even integers is as great as the number of all the integers (even and odd) of the entire set or collection of natural numbers. This numerical equivalence in its totality is designated by Cantor as a "transfinite number." Transfinite numbers appear to obey rules of a logic foreign to the logic of finite numbers. And this is just the beginning. From such logic there arises a whole series of rules for the Cantorian infinities, rules foreign to the logic of Euclid.

I am in no way a follower of Rorty, rather my thinking is rooted in the realm of "metaphysics" much in tune with the idealism of Josiah Royce, who has offered one of the best conceptualizations of Cantor's actual infinities or, as Royce called them, "determinate infinities"[4]. Puzzled, I have found it difficult to sort out the pros and cons of Cantor's argumentation and form a coherent judgment. During his lifetime, and still today, Cantor's theses provoked hefty discussion among mathematicians and philosophers regarding the coherency and legitimacy of Cantor's actual infinities. In the ensuing discussion, I shall cut the Gordian knot by (a) offering definitions of potential and actual infinities, (b) explaining the meaning of the definitions as so constructed, and (c) finally offering a few remarks on the integrity (or lack of it) of the logic of infinite numbers as exemplifications of actual infinity.

II. Definition of Potential Infinity

Definition: Seriality without a principle of finality, viz., termination, or succinctly put, seriality without end.

The ensuing analysis takes as its point of departure the physicist George Gamow who supposedly summarized the nature of the problem of counting with: "One, two, three, infinity'. A more traditional representation would be "1, 2, 3, ...," a symbolization that communicates an equivalent numerical expression of infinity within the series of natural numbers. The three dots are superior to the symbol ∞. A translation of Gamow's verbalization into 1, 2, 3, ..., ∞ seems odd and misleading. Such a symbolization, if at all sensible, would imply that infinity is a number, an infinite number. This form of symbolization obviously prejudices the argument as to the status of ∞ as a number (or not). The use of three (or more) dots constitutes an excellent formula for a series that is potentially infinite. In place of the three (or more) dots one can find expressions such as "etc, etc., etc." "so on and so on" or even, "and so on, infinitely". Nevertheless, the three dots or its equivalents do suggest an on-going-ness, a continuation of more and more (*ad infinitum*) without any final numerical value being specified or even specifiable. The series of natural numbers would seem to imply *qua* its structural seriality an ever ongoing and expanding serialization which is, on principle, without a final end value. With regard to the given definition, we can also make the following points.

A series of natural numbers obtains the coherency of order by being serialized according to a rule of reiterative production. In the case of the serialization of natural numbers this rule is designated, for simplification, as a principle of unit-augmentation, i.e., the subsequent number is always one unit greater than its immediately previous one. Of supreme importance here, is the insight that the basic principle of unit-augmentation-serialization contains in its essential organization absolutely no principle (rule or formula) that enables or entails an obligatory conclusion, finality, termination or end to the further augmentation of the serialization. Potential infinity by the very nature of its seriality includes, generates, enables, entails no end, i.e., it is without end! In this context, the Latin formulation of *ad infinitum* properly applies to potential infinity. The prefix "ad-" means "towards" or ' approaching," but not "reaching" or "arriving at." If infinity is to claim the status of a number, then the series can and must reach (arrive at) a specific numerical value that enacts a structural closure of the series. If not, there can be no totality of all the numbers serialized. In the case of arrival at a numerical value, i.e. an infinite number, the Latin variant (occasionally used) would be *"in infinitum."* Here *"in"* entails the meaning of "entering into", i.e., the series would culminate by entering or passing into (arriving at) actual infinity as a determinate number; just as 3 in the expanding serialization enters into and arrives at the next highest determinate number, i.e., becomes 4. If the counter follows the rule or formula of unit-augmentation, then infinity too must be conceived of as an actual number. Morris Lazerowitz has discussed critically the attempt to render ∞ as just another number.[5] His insights have influenced my current reflections on this topic — we can turn to them now.

A natural number is in essence at least a precise answer to the quantitative question: "How many?" There are a large number of books in any university library. In the case of each such library, one can ask: "Just how many?". Given agreement as to what constitutes a book, a questioner can expect as an answer a specific, exact, determinate and definite value, once all the books have been counted. This means that the "number" of books evinces of necessity an "end" number such that the collection of books *qua* a set entails completeness, entirety or totality — all properties inexorably absent in potential infinity. A so-called "number-without-end" cannot possess such completeness and, by its very definition (given above), it is structurally so. In other words, one answer is not logically valid, namely: "The number of books in the library is the precisely determinate number-without-end." This is not a quantitative answer to the question: "Just how many books are there?" The "without-end" means structurally that one more unit can potentially succeed any given value of n. In other words, given any n, there is of necessity a successor S(n). Potential infinity means that unit-augmentation constitutes the structure of the numerical series, and nothing more! This "nothing more" follows from the essence of serialization of natural numbers as the to-be-counted. The series evinces the property of being without end, not because the counter can temporally never arrive at its final member, but because its very essence is without end.

The definition given above and illustrated by the use of three or more dots is derived from considering "infinity" in terms of the finite or, in anticipation, of the finite positivity of things of the world of finitude. The essential point is that infinity is conceived extrapolatively in terms of a series of finite elements, an infinite set of collected numerical things. There is a relationship between infinity and finitude, or, as I prefer to express it: finitude entails homogeneity. In other words, the connection between infinity and finitude resides in the extrapolative nature of serialization. In the extrapolative relation between a series of finite things (objects or numbers) and an unending series of such "somethings" is expressed by the "in-" prefacing **in**finity: This prefix "in-" does not antithetically separate infinity from finitude, rather it unites them into a continuously extrapolating a homogeneity. I shall argue below that the relation between finitude and infinity is heterogeneous. Be that as it may, let me first introduce some reflections on the problem of a positive conceptualization of infinity.

It is not possible to define anything purely in terms of pure negativity, i.e., to determine what something is not. Positivity must pertain to anything and everything to be defined as something, or no definition is possible. But to define means to capture something conceptually by means of the intelligibility of the said thing to be defined within rational confines (limits), viz., *fines*. All this has consequences.

The main consequence is that the definition of potential infinity semantically borrows, appropriates, acquires its positivity by focusing upon the specific positivity of each and every n as the n's (NB not "all" the n's) are serialized into the series of natural numbers. Potential infinity derives its very intelligibility by relating its seeming negativity (its "in-'") to finitude in accord with a rule whereby the positivity of finite things (e.g., natural numbers) are ordered into an extrapolating sequence without end. In short, the positivity entailed in the definition of potential infinity is rooted in the structural possibility of augmenting without end the finite positivity of numbers of different quantitative values. This fundamental structure entails an essential property: the attribute of being "without end." This utterly excludes completeness, wholeness, entirety, all-ness or totality! Such properties do not pertain to the infinite *qua* potentiality. Because infinity transcends the positivity of the finitude (limits, boundaries, finalities) of numbers, its semantics depend upon extrapolating those numbers to the ultimate limit, which however turns out not to be because it is without end. Paradoxically the limit of potential infinity is limitless, and nothing more. A problem arises when we attempt to consider that potential infinity as a whole, i.e., as actual. This problem will be the object of the definition of actual infinity.

Let me stress that the positivity of actual infinity will entail enormous if not insuperable difficulties. In itself the borrowed positivity of potential infinity in no way reveals what infinite positivity is in itself, let alone how conceptually to approach such positivity. Without positivity, any definition of actual infinity will become nothing for conceptual comprehension. It does not suffice to claim that infinity is not finitude. Such a definition would reveal no more than an "is not,' rather than a "what is." To grasp this matter, it is necessary to turn to actual infinity, which we will in turn also need to "define". But before attempting to define actual infinity, I would like to emphasize the fact that the definition I shall suggest will differ from the ones found in almost all works consulted.

III. Definition of Actual Infinity

As a short preface to actual infinity, let me state that I will attempt to offer one definition of actual infinity with three mutually supplementary aspects or, one might say, a triune definition constituting the complexity of the full definition. One definition will be negative, the next positive and the last will entail the docta ignorantia as the final word on infinite positivity. This third sub-definition will lead to the conclusion that (1) the inquirer knows that there actually is infinite positivity, and (2) that he or she cannot on principle have any knowledge whatsoever about what this positivity is in itself; yet (3) the inquirer does know learnedly that all is to be so. Once having "defined" actual infinity, I shall assert some theses concerning actual infinity in mathematics and finally in theology, and end with more questions than solutions. It should be noted in advance that Nicholas of Cusa's reflections on infinity as interpreted with ample profundity by Mariano Álvarez Gómez[6] will constitute the methodological background to the ensuing theses. This will be quite obvious from the Latin terminology. (With literary license, this study can be viewed as an enacted duel between Cusa and Cantor.)

Actual infinity:

(a) Negative Definition: ∞ = *fines-non-habens; seu non-aliud esse*
(b) Positive Definition: ∞ = *ultra coincidentiam oppositorum* (or transition from negativity to pure positivity)
(c) Self-Abolishing Definition:
∞ = *docta ignorantia ineffabile positive*

Let us begin with definition (a): Actual infinity excludes in all absoluteness any limits, parts, multiplicity, plurality or, in short, manifoldness. Actual infinity is absolute relative to finitude in the sense that "absolute" means "cut off from." This methodological approach is in total opposition to the one used for interpreting potential infinity, which begins with the finite and extrapolates to the infinite, always "beyond" any given finite limit reached. Finitude essentially belongs to potential infinity. The impertinence of finitude to actual infinity is, so to speak, the standpoint from which actual infinity receives its intelligibility. Simply put: potential infinity includes finitude as a necessary homogeneous feature of its definition, whereas actual infinity heterogeneously excludes finitude from its essential definition.

It is in terms of this exclusionary feature that the positivity of actual infinity will acquire some learned clarity and enable a partial insight into its specific nature. For the moment it suffices to note that definition (a) permits no limitation of any sort as pertaining to actual infinity and, as will be claimed, indicates the nature of its positivity. It is also to be noted that the absence of manifoldness in actual infinity means that ∞ cannot answer the quantitative question: "Just how many are there?" This automatically nullifies any attempt to consider ∞ as just another number serialized in the endless sequence of natural numbers. No number can possess the property of "without end" which defines potential infinity. Moreover, because of the total exclusion of manifoldness in actual infinity, it can be maintained that said infinity evinces absolute simplicity. Such an exclusionary property offers insights into infinite simplicity, viz., the simplicity of infinity. The conclusion here is logically derived from definition (a). This means that any adequate analysis of actual infinity should focus upon what is meant by *fines-non-habens*.

In order to render definition (b) comprehensible it is necessary to examine again the series of natural numbers, a series without end, i.e., *ad infinitum*. In doing this, one obtains the notion of positivity *per se*, namely that of each finite thing or, in this case, of numbers. As noted above, nothing can be defined solely in terms of negativity. In defining potential infinity, positivity was grasped by focusing upon the "whatness" of each and every n (or anything) and subsequently serializing such numbers in order to generate a notion of extrapolative (potential) infinity as a series without end. Such conceptualization took place because I, being of quite finite intellect, began with the only positivity accessible. In order to grasp actual infinity, focus must be shifted from serialization, i.e., the dynamics of augmenting a sequence, to the structural nature of the series itself conceived as a unitary thing (or set). Some questions follow:

But what enables the series, as opposed to the serialization, to be "what" it is? A numerical series with or without end is evinced in its structural differentiation (plurality) and organization (unification of plurality). Examining the numerical series, it becomes evident that certain distinct, yet oppositional features (*opposita*), structure its seriality. These properties are the mutually supplementary opposites of identity and difference, sameness and otherness, unity and diversity, oneness and multiplicity, or for the purpose of this discussion, positivity and negativity. Let us sketch out this thesis in more detail.

Sameness and otherness formally belong to each separate number of the series of numbers if such a series is to be *per se*. Each number (n) in the unique unicity of its quantitative specificity fuses fully with the otherness of the unique unicity of any other numerical specificity taken serially. In this way sameness and otherness are *opposita* which generate a sequential *coincidentia* that establishes the very specific numericity of each and every number within the seriality of natural numbers. Of more importance are the *opposita* of positivity and negativity. Without positivity and negativity there can be no serialized multiplicity or manifoldness. Thereby arises the multiplicity without which the necessary juxtaposition which organizes seriality would be impossible. The sameness of each number n includes a specific positivity that excludes (negates or invalidates) the very otherness of the specific positivity of any and each of the other numbers taken in seriality. Inclusion (positivity) is intrinsically blended, fused or smelted together to the exclusion of all others. Positivity and negativity are in structure fully and formally fused/amalgamated in each materially different number *qua* finitude. The fusion/amalgamation of opposing features in each number can be terminologically designated as *coincidentia*. Each number as a type of anything materially entails its own proper positivity (specific quantity) which distinguishes it from the proper positivity (specific quantity) of each and any other number, yet relates it and any others together as seriality. In short, each number (or anything) is constituted by oppositional duality of sameness and otherness wherein the sameness mediates its otherness to the otherness of the sameness of any other number. At this point it becomes imperative to focus upon the meaning of definition (b) in order to progress to the "learned" identification of "ignorance" with the ineffable positivity of actual infinity alluded to in definition (c), thereby "answering" the question as to what the "*ultra*" means in (b).

Positivity and negativity as with all other *opposita* coincide in order to constitute the finite specificity of each number. In order words, positivity and negativity formally represent a certain *coincidentia oppositorum*. A serialization of numbers proceeds in its augmentative dynamics onward structurally without end. From here one can derive the semantic core of an understanding of potential infinity. Correlatively, any finite or infinite series conceived structurally is constituted by the *coincidentia oppositorum*. But, it should be clearly noted, the term *coincidentia* itself implies a certain confluence, concurrence of coming together, all of which imply merged duality. But as definition (a) ascertains, actual infinity lacks all duality (plurality, manifoldness, limits or finality). This is what is meant by claiming that infinity exhibits the feature of *esse non-aliud*. All this derives from the property of *fines-non-habens*. Simply put, in actual infinity there is absolutely no duality, even as *coincidentia oppositorum*. Whereas the doctrine of *coincidentia oppositorum* is quite adequate for potential infinity, it cannot conceptually mediate to human intelligence the full positivity of actual infinity, though it leads thinking to such positivity. Human intelligence can only capture the positive "whatness" of things. What is this fullness of the positivity of actual infinity which by necessity remains opaque?

That there is ∞ *pure and simple* (*schlechthin*) derives by necessity from considering the extrapolative nature of endless serialization. The notion of "without end" remains problematic, incomplete and open ended. Whence does the endlessness of potential infinity derive its semantics? The "without end" of potential infinity inexorably imparts the impulse to conceive and consider the "without end" in some way as a full totality, viz., entirety. Potential infinity that illuminates, however, darkly, seriality seems to imply conceptually a non-serial wholeness and fullness in purity, a purity beyond (*"ultra"*) the *coincidentia oppositorum* of endless finitude. "Endless" is not a self-sustaining negative concept. It needs positivity to inform its "less an end."

By writing "purity" the attempt Is made to indicate that ∞ in itself is positivity (sameness, identity, unicity) without any negativity (otherness, difference, multiplicity) whatsoever. Pure positivity leads inexorably to the *ultra coincidentiam oppositorum*. The very simplicity of actual infinity demands such an *"ultra"* lest it be left in the merging duality in the *coincidentia* which orders seriality. Expressed differently, the conceptualization of potential infinity entails the oppositional properties of positive/negative, sameness/difference, unicity/divergence. The *"ultra"* or "beyond" the structurally inclusive *coincidentia oppositorum* seeks to capture actual infinity as excluding all duality, even that contained in the oppositional coincidence of potential infinity. Actual infinity is *fines-non-habens*! The thesis just presented is derived as a logical conclusion and, hence, is learned knowledge.

But—and here commences ignorance—it is immediately evident that the very reasoning that leads to the doctrine of "ultra *coincidentiam oppositorum*"' leaves the inquirer in complete and total obliviousness as to what such positivity without negativity means. The rational inquirer is left in complete ignorance. The thinker does not even possess the minimal knowledge of what positivity *pure and simple* might mean. Conceptually, semanticity is totally absent. The insight into the *"ultra"* reveals that I possess absolutely non-knowledge, viz., ignorance about that to which the *"ultra"* points. Everything is blank, full of ineffability, empty of semantics. Ignorance is utterly total. However, such ignorance constitutes precisely the logically reasoned ignorance of the meaning of the *"ultra"*' For this reason it represents docta *ignorantia* and bids the thinker to modesty. Pure positivity is not the simplicity that is the absence of complexity, which is the meaning usually associated with the term. On the contrary, such pure positivity is in actual infinity absolutely rich, abundant, utterly full, yet without the complexity of multiplicity entailed in finite richness. What absolute abundance without complexity means is beyond any and all knowledge, save that of an actually infinite consciousness. Ultra-abundance is just as opaque as actual infinity being nothing other than an aspect thereof. Though the inquirer possesses absolutely no knowledge of what the pure positivity of actual infinity means, he or she does most rationally know that things in their serialized potential infinity lead with logical necessity to the reality of such "beyondness." This constitutes human *docta ignorantia* and thereby all the *sapientia* in such matters.

A paradoxical remark: The inquirer's knowledge of positivity derives from his acquaintance with finitude which produces in English the rubric "thing". "Thingness" provides the thinker with insight into the positivity of its intelligibility and thereby the comprehension of its positivity. By means of insight into things (anything, something, everything and, yes, nothing) one has access to the knowledge that there is positivity and just what this term can mean (or not). Human knowledge commences by confronting a world of "things," all of which possess *per* definitionem: *fines-habens*. Infinity in itself entails accordingly *non-aliud esse*. Consequently, infinity qua actuality is per its definitional property beyond things, viz., it excludes "'thingness". Infinity is no thing, no-thing, nothing. Nothing can mean the total absence of things. At best this is a limit-concept that cannot be fully realized without contradiction. It is clear that this is not the meaning here intended. The intended meaning is that "thingness" does not belong, viz., pertain to infinity, all of which reveals that infinity is beyond thingness thereby making it no thing, no-thing or nothing. This thesis could have disturbing implications for much traditional theology that conceives of God as "*ens infinitum*" since "*ens*" is just a Latin expression for "thing". In short, God *qua* being infinite is nothing! Such a thesis is getting ahead of the analysis. It suffices to assert that, mathematically considered, infinity is no number! A few conclusions will now be drawn from the above theoretical discussion.

IV. Some Critical Remarks Concerning Infinity as Numerically Actual

In order to focus and simplify the ensuing comments I shall briefly trace Lieber's transformation of potential infinity into actual infinity. Lieber's analysis certainly constitutes a conceptual simplification. Nevertheless, its very simplicity captures the absolute minimum which appeals in one form or the other in conceptualizations of actual infinity. Lieber[7] (2007: 77) conceives of "potential" infinity as being something which is approached but never reached. Consider now the positive integers, i.e., the whole numbers, like 1, 2, 3, etc. Instead of writing "etc." so soon, you can of course continue the sequence as far as you please and then follow it by dots like this: . . . to indicate that this sequence is approaching ∞. But, if you consider this sequence as a whole you have an illustration of an "Actual" infinity [emphasis mine].

For the moment, the falsity of claiming that one can by counting approach, though never reach, infinity will be only briefly touched upon. Lieber has caught, however confusedly, the essence of potential infinity. Unfortunately, she confounds the acts of counting with the to-be-counted. The counter never reaches ∞ not because of any time considerations, rather because the series to be counted is in and of itself structurally without end. This has become evident in the above discussion of numerical serialization. Numbers as the to-be-counted, not the counting of them, are structurally endless. Time plays no role whatsoever, even in the adverbial form of never. In addition it is incorrect to maintain that the augmenting series of numbers "approach" infinity. Given that potential infinity is without end, there is no vantage point from which the nearness or distance to being without end can be measured and hence numerically quantified. All that can be maintained is that as numbers augment unit for unit, they become ever more distant from the first integer of the relevant series. In potential infinity, there is no measurable approaching infinity, only increasing remoteness from the initial integer.

The result is that Lieber lacks an adequate definition of potential infinity. She is, to be sure, not alone. Moreover, the operative term is "consider"? The reader is asked to consider a potentially infinite serialization as a closed off whole. This is an inadequate formulation since the verb "to consider" can mean merely "to believe to be so". One can believe Lenin's materialism to have been inspired by the Virgin Mary in a dream. But one cannot realize such a "'consideration" with any degree of plausibility. To justify a specific "to consider to be," one must envisage the two terms related through said consideration to be conceivable as being plausibly together. I shall directly attempt to conceive of the transformation of potential infinity into actual infinity as Lieber's hypothetical "consider" so requires.

(1) First of all, it is necessary to grasp the central meaning of a group of interrelated terms that mesh together with the notion of a "whole". Let us say that there are five books strewn across my desk. One can count all said books in their entirety so as to ascertain the sum totality to be set as an ordered whole upon the neighboring bookshelf. Terms such as "all", "entirety", "totality" and "whole" are all interrelated concepts. In the context of the series of natural numbers such terms are only applicable to closed off, finished or determinate quantities of finite members in a numerical set, as in this case of the set of books on the shelf. All such terms obtain their rationality and applicability only in having reference to units of

finitude; that is, they belong to the realm of finitude. From this fact a central question presents itself.

Is the application of such interrelated terms, subsumed under the, notion of "whole" to an endless serialization of natural numbers *qua* potential infinity at all conceivable? Or is such an equation on the same level of Lenin's Virgin Mary materialism? What is a thinker required to do conceptually, if he or she is to "consider" a series without end to, be a series constituting a whole, totality, entirety in which all members are present (or can be generated according to a rule terminating as an ultimate completed finality, viz., consummated infinity)? The very formulation of the question inexorably suggests a contradiction as an answer. In other words, such an equation of an endless series with an infinitely completed serialized whole entails a logical incongruity. Lieber's imperative to "consider" forces anyone who follows such advice to affirm a theoretical oxymoron and then to ignore the paradox. But only by means of such ignoring can Lieber obtain a method to finitize infinity, i.e., to apply finite math to infinity thereby transforming it into an "as if" infinite number. So far, I have read no one who offers a single example of a series which is actually infinite. Potentially infinite, yes. Actually infinite, no. In other words, the symbolization of a potentially infinite series is proffered and then simply treated as a whole or totality. So arises an infinite number. Let us consider Lieber's suggested illustration[8] of the numerical equivalence between natural and even numbers:

> Now let us go back to the "actually" infinite set of positive integers. You will soon see that it has a remarkable property that no finite set ever has! For you will agree that all the even integers (2, 4, 6, etc.) are contained in this set, thus being a part of the entire set:-of positive integers (both even and odd). And yet let us now compare the following two sets: (1) the set of all integers: 1, 2, 3, 4, 5,... (2) the set of even integers only: 2, 4, 6, 8,10 (...). Hence there is a 1 - 1 correspondence between the members of sets (1) and (2) (...) and consequently these two sets are "equivalent", that is, they each have the same number of members ... [emphasis mine].

If I take the set of all the integers: 1, 2, 3, 4, 5..., I discover that all the numbers are not illustrated as a consummated whole, as *infinitum in actu*. What one has is a formula for the potentially endless serialization of natural numbers *ad infinitum*, i.e., toward potential infinity, but not actually reaching or actually arriving *in infinitum*, i.e., at an actual infinity. The dots after the given numbers indicate that the series goes on and on without end, and nothing more. This property was derived from the above definition of potential infinity. Lieber wants to consider two series without end as numerically equivalent to completed wholes or, simply, as possessing the same number of numerical members. What Lieber cannot do is to conceive as free of contradiction the equivalence between two series without end as possessing the same number of numerical members.

No real discussion is offered, just consideration. Just how one can conceive a structurally endless series as numerically ended and thereby constituting a "whole" proper of the realm of finitude, all this is not evident. Indeed, it appears that a contradiction has been considered as a non-contradiction! An example of such incongruity can readily be seen in Ardián Paenza, who offers "the natural numbers (all)" as an example of actual infinity[9]. In no way does "all" have meaning for a series of numbers without end! The mathematician can validly assert theses concerning "any" number of an endless serialization, but not about "all" of them, i.e., not without asserting a very incongruous contradiction by surreptitiously introducing wholeness, viz., totality, viz., allness into potential infinity. Lieber, along with other proponents of Cantorian math, simply aver the completion of the structutally extrapolating series of natural numbers. In this way they concoct a fascinating mathematics of completed series without end!

(2) The attempt to metamorphize potential infinity into actual infinity reveals itself to entail a logical incongruity. Infinity is theorized methodologically within the framework of an endless extrapolation of the "things" called natural numbers augmentatively ordered serially. I fail completely to gain an insight into the logical intelligibility of such a metamorphosis and remain unconvinced by the discussions pursued up till now. The method of conceptualization used has included infinity within the confines of the serialized things of finitude. Infinity is conceived as an extrapolative function of finitude. In short, infinity and finitude are viewed as homogeneously related. In the definition of actual infinity given above, the methodology was reversed. Infinity was considered conceptually under the auspices of the exclusion of all finitude from its essence. The starting point of the attempted triune definition given above is *fines-non-habens*. In other words, infinity is conceived of as excluding all finitude. In short, the relation of infinity to finitude is one of heterogeneity. Since terms such as whole, entirety, totality and allness possess validity only for the realm of finitude, they do not at all pertain to actual infinity. Actual infinity cannot be consequently integrated into a series of finitudes or, in this study, of numbers. A number is "in itself" finite. For this reason, a plurality of such finitudes can be organized according to wholeness, entirety, totality and allness. Actual infinity prohibits such assimilation to the interrelated concepts of whole, etc. Actual infinity thereby is not applicable to mathematical organization. Even if the consideration of a potentially infinite series could legitimately be subsumed under the rubrics of whole, entire, etc., such a whole would in no way be actually infinite. More to the point, such finitized potential infinities would (and in fact do) effectively constitute mini-infinities, an oxymoron par excellence. This

is an out and out contradiction! What relation can actual infinity evince relative to numerical finitude?

If actual infinity is to have a relation to numerical finitude, such a relation should be developed from a consideration of what function can be derived from pure positivity. Some fruitful ideas can be found in Cusa. Certainly, the notion of *coincidentia oppositorum* constitutes one possibility. In this context I can recommend Mariano Álvarez Gómez's discussion of the *coincidentia* and infinitude[10]. The result of my reflections is that actual infinity is no number and may not validly be used to concoct a mathematics of infinity of (actual) infinities.

(3) As an ultimate finale to the mathematical ramifications, I submit that the very moment of departure for this study accepted an implicit confusion. The "infinities" of actual infinity and potential infinity have been treated separately, whereas they are fully synonymous. The examination of infinity, neither actual nor potential, is the center of this, study! Whether infinity is actual or not is conceptually of secondary importance. The above definition of actual infinity is in reality a definition of infinity *per se*. Whether such a definition implies or not *in actu* or *in potentia* plays no immediate role in the construction of the definition. The question that arises concerns the licitness of a Cantorian totalization of an endless series. Can one validly consider potential infinity to be closed as a totality, viz., whole? An affirmative answer implies a homogeneous relationship between finitude and infinity, i.e., infinity is an extrapolation of finitudes serialized. The definition of actual infinity proffered has called into question the assumption of homogeneity. Such a relation is now seen as false, i.e., within the framework of the definitions given.

I started my analysis with the thesis that infinity and finitude are heterogeneously connected, and I sought, in the light of such heterogeneity, to ascertain what is conceptually entailed in considering infinity, when taken in itself, to be exclusive of all finitude. Mathematically, the very conception of a series without end entails that potential infinity is. In mathematics, what is conceived, *is* - which is a form of the ontological argument. But the "infinity" of potential infinity receives its semi-opaque positivity by extrapolating according to a rule from ordered numerical finitudes without end and then projecting such extended positivity upon the series thereby constituting its very being (or *esse*). Factually, this is a variant of the ontological argument. What is conceived possesses to that degree being, viz., *esse*. But the property of being without end on the part of the infinity of potential infinity is just a truncated form of infinity *per se*, i.e., it delineates what infinity can be when related homogeneously to finitude. Taken heterogeneously, actual infinity is *qua* being conceptualized as pure positivity. However, for this reason it is not a number. Does such a conceptualization imply reality beyond (*ultra*) being a concept? If so, the ontological argument extends beyond mathematical being to being as such. Of importance for this final remark is that infinity used in terms of potentiality does not englobe the full positivity pertaining to infinity *per se*, being reduced to a "without end." But being without end is not an adequate conceptualization of infinity *per se*. This inadequacy has led - I surmise - to the attempt to totalize endless finitude into a full infinity. The result has been a refined finitization of infinity in a sort of finite math of infinities. In this way, that which excludes the very plural finitudes necessary for serialization, namely infinity, has become open to numerically finite manipulation. This feat is achieved at the cost of blurring the positivity of infinity *per se*. Hence the need to introduce the distinction between potential and actual infinity. In short, the full meaning revealed in the *docta ignorantia ineffabile positiva* is lost and infinity becomes a serialization without end. One is left to debate whether endless seriality can be ended, viz., considered a totality.

V. Some Theological Ramifications

The methodological principle deriving from and grounding the above definition of infinity *per se* is the distinction between an extrapolative and exclusionary approach to the conceptualization of infinity, be it potential or actual. Mathematically it has been contended that the extrapolative method leads to the contradictory endeavor that seeks to close off, make whole, totalize, i.e., to finitize the endless "without end" of "potential" infinity and thereby to transform the extrapolation "less an end" into an "actual" infinity, a supposed number now open mathematically to finite manipulation. This method treats finitude and infinity as homogeneously related. Indeed. homogeneity is the essential component of extrapolative structure. In this way infinity takes on quite finite features, one of which is to treat ∞ as just another n. This faulty equivalence has, as noted above, been severely criticized by Laserowitz[11], who considers an infinite number to be just an "as if" number. For Laserowitz this is a patent absurdity, no matter how magnificent the mathematic manipulation of said "as if" number(s) might be. The same fundamental tension is manifest in two conflictive approaches to theology relative to the affirmation (or denial) of properties to God qua infinity, namely in theologies that both conceptually use the extrapolative method in pursuing affirmation of attributions to God. And such a pursuit is historically the most disseminated mode of reflection on infinity in Christianity. I shall briefly, though critically, examine the positive (*cataphatic*) and negative (*apophatic*) schools of affirmation, first in the person of the Thomist, Fernand van Steenberghen[12], and, second, in the person of the Russian Orthodox theologian, Vladimir Lossky[13]. The tortuous tension between finitude and infinity depicted above will be clearly evinced in both theological modes of conceptualizing divinity. Once the critical presentation has been completed, I will sketch out a few suggestions for a third way based upon the exclusionary approach to infinity, the one used in the above definition of actual infinity and derived from Nicholas of Cusa. Cusa's exclusionary method rests upon the heterogeneity between finitude and infinity.

(1) In the consideration of finite units (numbers or entities) it is evident that numerical units have a relation of one to another. Indeed, such a relation implies proportionality. One might well view math as a study of proportionalities. The extrapolative thinker who seeks to conceive of infinity as a totalization, viz., as completion of potentially endless finitude and, thereby, to generate an actual infinite number or, metaphysically, an infinity (entity, viz., Being) justifies her or his affirmations by establishing proportionalities between numbers (entities) and infinity. Numerical proportionality between n and ∞ is carried over into theological ontology by affirming that finite being(s) is (are) analogous to infinite Being. Thomists such as Steenberghen seek to connect the extrapolative nature of numbers with the extrapolative nature, of entities by means of the doctrine of the analogy of being(s). This leads Steenberghen to seek a "real" ontological proportionality between (ontic) finitude and divine infinity by means of a causal argument that denies that, ontologically, causality can be potential, viz., without end, though not denying that mere sequentiality can be such. Such a denial is the conceptual means that positive attributers use to close off any endless regression of sequentiality relative to "real"'' beings. I have no interest in, judging the cogency of a Thomistic proof of divine existence by means of a causal argument. It suffices to note that, once an endless sequence of causes has been, so to speak, capped, viz., closed off, it implies an ontologically actual whole, i.e., "'an infinite Being?" as absolute cause. Within the context of the real causal dependency of finite being(s) upon a non-caused Absolute reality, Steenberghen justifies the principle "that the perfection of an effect pre-exists eminently in its cause"[15]. Analogy is made to engender proportionality between finitude and infinity by claiming that the proportionality concerned is one of "eminence"? Such eminence is supposed to result in the establishment of a real ontological proportionality between finite being(s) and "an Infinite Being" The difficulty in extrapolating in positive theology can be highlighted by the notion of "eminence" which is, I maintain, the indispensable "jack-up-clause," viz., totalization of a "consideration" (cf. Lieber above) that transforms endless seriality (= potential infinity) into actually being a whole of infinity, called God. In reality "eminence" remains metaphorically opaque, covering up a lack of conceptual clarity. The Thomistic conceived divine Being is in intent absolutely transcendent of, and, hence, heterogeneous to (finite) being(s), yet it stands in a homogenous proportionality to finite being. This is, indeed, a problematic tension, if not a semantic duality, one that I shall try to illuminate by focusing upon the peculiar ambiguity of Steenberghen's. formulation of God qua infinity.

In his list of ontological conclusions, Steenberghen defines God as the "Absolute" in the following manner: "L'absolu 'est un Être infini"(1952, 259). Steenberghen's French has been used because there is an ambiguity in the French "un" that bifurcates in English into "an" and "one." Steenberghen has maintained in English: 'The Absolute is an (or one) infinite Being" Whether "an" or "one" is meant (and I maintain that both ate amorphously implied), Steenberghen is applying the properties of numericity, e.g., 1, 2, 3, ..., to (actual) infinity *qua* being. Without doubt there are not two or more beings qua infinity that are divine, viz., God. To claim a plurality of Gods qua infinity would be illicitly to apply a finite category, namely numericalness, to that which excludes all pertinence of finitude to infinity proper. My exclusionary definition of actual infinity means that finitude, whatsoever is heterogeneously foreign to infinity, is excluded from infinity. Infinity means definitionally *fines-non-habens*. Logically it follows that even to affirm in a positive manner that there is one or a God qua infinity, is to finitize God and not adequately to affirm what follows from exclusionary "Being Infinitely" (*esse infinite*). The formulation just used allows for no plurality of *Being* (*esse*), hence there is no valid application of numericity, viz., numbers to God. Not even the number "one! To affirm one of a God *qua* infinity is a valid linguistic means of excluding polytheism, but only a means, since numericity is not affirmable of God *per se*. To affirm one or a God *qua* infinity is a mode of speaking. Although at times of use, it nevertheless remains logically a deficient *modus significandi* of the exclusionary nature of God *qua* infinity. Such deficiency is evident in Steenberghen's formulations which we will now briefly examine.

Steenberghen's conceptualization of God according to proportionality with finite being(s) transforms Infinite Being into a possible recipient of finitizing numericity. This constitutes a threat to the heterogeneous integrity of divine transcendence. I claim that even to affirm that God *qua* infinity is one or a, is unintentionally to finitize God into the subject of quite finite attributions, all of which leads to the ambiguity of "un Être infini" It subsequently becomes necessary to prove that there cannot be two or more exemplifications of "un Être infini." This leaves the Absolute as a function of an extrapolative "more or less," indeed, as a hybrid of "more/less," viz., "infini/un." The positive version of the extrapolatory conceptualization of infinity leaves God as an amalgam, part "un" and part "infini." The heterogeneity of Infinity has been lost in a vague conceptualization of "eminence." Let us now turn to the negative method of extrapolative theology.

(2) Positive theology commences with the endless extrapolative augmentation of finitude and concludes with actual infinity. Based on this positive connection, it attempts to conclude from the properties of finite being to positive knowledge about infinite Being, relative to which said properties are affirmed as eminently present, all the while without being able to conceive adequately what "eminence"

means. Negative theology, on the other hand, is the mirror image of positive extrapolation, accepting without question the extrapolatively conceptualized relation between finitude and infinity, only denying that any property of finitude can be extrapolatively affirmed of God *qua* infinity because the disparity between the two realms is absolute. As is evident from my definition of actual infinity, I find negative theology to be a significant improvement over positive theology. At any rate, acutely aware of such ontological dissimilarity, negative theology is forced to conceptualize God as *Deus absconditus*, which is, Lossky asserts, "the apophatic foundation of all true theology"[16]

The "hiddenness" of God in Christian thought is not new and is even found in positive theology. Negative theology, however, radically denies to reason any access or penetration whatsoever into such divine concealment, thus leaving God structurally in the "ténèbres divines," viz., "divine darkness." Indeed, Lossky asserts that "apophatism is thus a criterion ... of the disposition of the spirit to the truth."[17] There is a paradox here that should be examined. Why?

Since the normal notion of truth means the rationally comprehended correspondence of what is affirmed with the to-be-known, negative theology seems to be maintaining that the truth (rationally known) is that there is no truth (rationally known) about God because God is "unknowable by nature?"[18] and this last thesis is evidently also "rationally known." As we will see, this will be a point of difficulty. In short, this "truth" seems to culminate, puzzlingly, in a cognitive nihilism which threatens to leave any being with reason in a Nietzschean world without God. Such a thesis must be investigated, for it reveals the strengths and labilities of negative theology.

It turns out that negative theologians do, indeed, reason and with enormous acuity, i.e., they critique most insightfully the unsustainable "consideration" which conceives the extrapolative derivation of actual infinity from finitude. Such a critique will not be followed here. I agree with it, but it suffices to note that the negative theologian affirms that any (rational) knowledge about God *qua* infinity in himself requires of the thinker "to deny all which is inferior (= finitude) to him" because finitude qua finitude remains infinitely removed from infinity. This disparity leaves said infinity in itself "in fundamental, absolute unknowableness." Consequently, the "unknowability of God is the sole definition proper of God."[19]

How does negative theology save rational beings from the despair of a *Deus absolute absconditus*, i.e., a God being beyond rational access *per se*? Lossky's powerfully emphatic reply is that Christianity is not a speculative school of philosophy about abstract concepts, but above all a communion with a living God?"[20] The assertion is not a matter of mere, let alone blind, faith. There is no fideism here!

Instead there is another source mediating access to God *qua* infinity. "God does not present Himself as an object to be known, because it is not a matter of knowledge, rather of union." By means of immediate union with the infinite or with God *qua* infinity, mysticism generates and grounds, according to Lossky, the theology of Russian Orthodoxy. "Negative theology is thus a way towards the mystical union with God whose nature remains unknown to us."[21]. Mystical union and the absolutely unknown are mutually reciprocal elements in negative theology. In other words, once the positive process of extrapolation from the finite to the infinite has been denied as an access to divine infinity, the negative theologian exhorts quite literally a leap beyond endless extrapolation of the finite into a mystical union with Divine infinity. This union is to be achieved in part by distracting human consciousness from all things finite, not only intellectually, but also ascetically, i.e., from the extrapolative breath of unending finitudes. "It is necessary to renounce to the senses as well as to reason, every object sensible or intelligible . . . with the purpose of being able to attain in absolute ignorance union with Him who surpasses every being and all science". Mysticism consequently advises that, "A purification, a *catharsis*, is necessary: one should abandon all which is impure and even things pure . . . It is only in this way that one penetrates the darkness (ténèbres) where there abodes He who is beyond all things".[22] The mystical way certainly offers the individual an immediate, direct and overpoweringly convincing experience of absoluteness or, more correctly formulated, incomprehensible infinity. Although such an encounter is not phenomenologically refutable, it is, nevertheless, limited to each and every individual experience. But it seems that many mystic practitioners often wish to convey this overwhelming experience to others. There are studies of the metaphorical and aesthetic language used by mystics to express their unitive encounter. However, all such "talk" is, alas, conceptually lacking in purely rational clarity. At this point, difficulties arise for systematic theology. Lossky quotes John Damascene who writes that "the Divine is infinite and incomprehensible and the only thing that we can understand is His infinity and incomprehensibility"[23]

It is at this point that a serious problematic originates in negative theology concerning the "whatness" of that which is being conceptualized. Negative theology abounds in the term "infinity" accompanied with the affirmation that the theologian is rationally in absolute ignorance of what this infinity is. However, when negative theology attempts to "understand" infinity, it applies the very exact same method that typifies the extrapolative affirmation in positive theology. What unites the positive and negative attempted "understanding" of infinity is the extrapolative method itself. In the final analysis, negative theology can assert no more than what infinity is not. Above it was noted that no definition of a referent is possible in purely negative terms. Without "positivity" the referred to is indistinguishable from a semantic nullity, i.e. it is meaningless. In other words, if the logic of negativity is followed, then even the affirmed "ignorance" of infinity itself cannot be comprehensibly avowed. This is so because negativity alone is not capable of conceptualizing the logical "object" referred to. Whereas negative theology avoids the deficient extension of finitude to infinity (clearly seen in Steenberghen's "un Être infini"), it cannot coherently even allude to the logical "object" of ignorance, so profusely denoted as infinity and, thereby, threatens to dissolve God *qua* infinity into semantic nonsense. In the last analysis even negative theology has to affirm something positive, viz., positivity in some way to infinity relative to which it can claim ignorance, that is if it is to have logical reference. If absolutely no positivity is entailed, then negative theology cannot fulfill its own imperative to "understand His infinity and incomprehensibility." It is just such an understanding that can be established by means of Nicholas of Cusa's exclusionary methodology which I have used above to conceptualize actual infinity.

(3) Negative theology seeks to "understand" God *qua* divine "infinity and incomprehensibility" This task is in my opinion the theological task *per se*, i.e., as far as philosophical theology is concerned. Positive theology is correct in its intent to affirm attributively positive content to divine infinity. However, it fails to achieve this task, not being able to free infinity in itself from the homogeneity of endless finitude. Negative theology is correct criticizing such attributions on the grounds of absolute and, hence, heterogeneous disparity between finitude and infinity. In this way, infinity liberated from extrapolative extension of finitude *ad infinitum*. However, negative theology does not transcend the extrapolative model underlying the very conceptual logic of denying the predication of finite attributes to infinity. The negation of finitude relative to infinity leads negative theology to assert that rational knowledge of said infinity is absolutely impossible, though, paradoxically, it affirmed that incomprehensible infinity "is" quite positively real. Negative theology, in its rational attempt to establish that infinite being is incomprehensible, conceptualizes extrapolatively, i.e., it uses an endlessly extrapolative series of "is not" affirmations. The, subsequent conception of God as infinite and incomprehensible fails at this point because negation alone can define absolutely nothing. "Nothing" as a limit concept implies the total absence of any positivity whatsoever. Such a denial taken to the limit dissolves or, indeed, annihilates itself, i.e., its very negating procedure also becomes nothing. This, paradoxically, makes the incomprehensibility asserted of infinity to be meaningless, to be a semantic blank. There can be no ignorance without some notion of the positivity of that which is not known or not even knowable. The absolute ignorance" of negative theology is absolutely ignorant and, therefore, not sustainable. I find, in opposition to and corrective of "absolute ignorance", conceptual adequacy in the "learned igno-

rance" of Cusa, a learnedness which encompasses a methodology for conceptualizing the "pure positivity" of (actual) infinity and for logically grounding its incomprehensibility. Following the exclusionary method the philosophical theologian can, indeed, obtain limited knowledge that avoids semantic vacuity, that is, that affirms the reality of infinity's positivity. In short, "pure" positivity can be positively affirmed to be, though it cannot be rationally comprehended qua being unadulterated positivity. Such pure positivity grounds the very logicity of ignorance of what the positivity of infinity is. This is accomplished because it presents a logically signified reference to which incomprehensibility itself can be attributed. The method of Cusa's conceptualizing was present in the definition of actual infinity given above and will not be repeated here. What is being done here its to determine how such a definition of actual infinity can have theological ramifications. What then is the difference between the methodologies of positive and negative theologies on one side and that of Cusa on the other?

The methodology of both positive and negative theology proceeds conceptually from the finite to the infinite, affirming or denying the homogeneous extension of finitude in infinitum. I have termed such methodology extrapolative, i.e., it compares the finite with the infinite *ad infinitum* and this means that finitude is introduced into that which excludes any comparison, thus producing confusion. Indeed, the discussion, as to whether there is one or more actual infinities already manifests logically the importation of finite categories into the conceptualization of actual infinity. In contrast, Cusa's methodology, which I have followed in my definition of actual infinity, is exclusionary, i.e., it seeks coherently to conceptualize actual infinity as that which excludes finitude or, conversely, finitude does not pertain to infinity *per se*. In order to justify this thesis, the triune principle of *coincidentia oppositorum* was applied to potential infinity leading to the notion of the *ultra coincidentiam oppositorum* of actual infinity. In this "beyond," the pure positivity of actual infinity is shown to be. Architectonic features of endlessly serialized finitude (i.e., potential infinity) coincide, becoming merged, fused, smelted together into the very "beyond" of pure positive identity. Such identity is conceptually derived from the categorical exclusion of finitude with its oppositional differentiation (positivity and negativity) from infinity (pure positivity). Infinity is no absolute mystery in opposition to finitude, rather a radical heterogeneity known as flowing from the emergence of oppositionality into a "beyond" of absolute positive identity. This positive identity, I repeat, derives from the categorical ousting of all finitude. Cusa's negation of finitude from infinity. This is the first step of exclusionary conceptualization and is followed, secondly, by the positive application of the principle of *"coincidentia"* leading to a learned understanding of the very incomprehensibility of ineffable infinite positivity. Divine of exclusionary method. On the contrary, it only offers a promising and grounded beginning. Since it is not the intent of this study to pursue such a "depth and width", this exposition will be brought to a close at this point. Instead, this study will end with the hope that the reader may have gained some conceptual clarity in thinking about infinity with references to its mathematical and theological ramifications - or if nothing else, at least an invitation to seek one's own conceptual clarification.

Footnotes

1 Manuel Cabada Castro, *Recuperar la infinitud: Entorno al debate histórico-filosófico sobre la limitation of ilimitación de la realidad*, (Madrid: Universidad Pontificia Comillas, 2008).

2 Millán-Puellas, Antonio, *Léxico Filsófico* (Madrid: Ediciones Rialp, 2002), 3-57.

3 Lilian R. Lieber, *Infinity. Beyond the Beyond the Beyond*, (Philadelphia: Paul Dry Books, 2007) 86, 226-229.

4 Josiah Royce, *The World and the Individual*, first series, *The Four Historical Conceptions of Being*, (Glouscester, Mass: Dover, 1976), 563-88.

5 Morris Lazerowitz, *The Language of Philosophy: Freud and Wittgenstein*, (Dordrecht: D. Reidel Publishing Company, 1977), 141-62-

6 Mariano Álvarez Gómez, *Pensamiento del ser y espera de Dios*, (Salamanca Ediciones Sígeme, 1968).

7 Lieber, *Infinity,* 77.

8 Ibid., 80.

9 Adrían Paenza, *Matemática, ¿estás ahí?,* (Barcelona: REA Libros, SA, 2005), 75.

10 Álvarez, *Pensamiento del ser y espera de Dios,* 13-42.

11 Laserowitz, *The Language of Philosophy. The Language of Philosophy: Freund and Wittgenstein,* (Dordrecht: D. Reidel Publishing Company, 1977).

12 Fernand van Steenberghen, *Ontologie*, (Louvain: Publications Universitaires de Louvain, 1952) 167-85-

13 Vladimir Lossky, *Essay sur la théologie mystique de L'Èglise d'Orient*, (Paris: Les Éditions du CERG, 1990), 21-41.

14 Steenberghen, *Ontologie*, 259

15 Ibid, 176.

16 Lossky, *Essay sur la théologie mystique de L'Ègise d'Orient*, 31.

17 Ibid., 37.

18 Ibid., 29

19 Ibid.

20 Ibid., 40.

21 Ibid., 2.

22 Ibid., 25.

23 Ibid., 3.

Bibliography

Álvarez Gómez, Mariano. *Pensamiento del ser y espera de Dios:* Salamanca, Ediciones Sígueme, 2004.

Cabada Castro, Manuel. *Recuperar la infinitude*: *Entorno al debate historico-filosófico sobre la limitación o ilimitación de la realidad*. Madrid: Commilas, 2008.

Lazerowitz, Morris. *The Language of Philosophy: Freud and Wittgenstein*. Dornrecht: D. Reidel Publishing Company, 1977.

Lossky, Vladimir. *Essay sur la théologie mystique de L'Èglise d'Orient*. Paris: Les Éditions du CERF. 1990.

Lieber, Lilian R. *Infinity Beyond the Beyond the Beyond*. Paul Dry Books, 2007.

Millán-Puelles, Antonio. *Léxico Filosófico*. Madrid: Ediciones RIALP, 2002.

Paenza, Adrían. *Matemática, ¿estás ahí?*. Barcelona: REA Libros, 2006.

Royce, Josiah. *The World and the Individual. First Series. The Four Historical Conceptions of Being*. Gloucester. ;ass- Dover, 1976.

Steenberghen, Ferdinand van. *Ontologie*. Louvain: Publications Universitaires de Louvain, 1952.

Chapter 4

The Ontological Argument
According to Josiah Royce

Abstract

In the 11th Century, St. Anselm constructed a proof of divine existence. Anselm's argument has had a long and notably influential history. Anselm seems to have proceeded from a mere consideration of the divine essence to the conclusion that God exists. Anselm's proof is considered by many to be the most audacious attempt in the history of philosophy. Anselm's mode of argumentation, generally rejected in the medieval period (e.g., by St Thomas Aquinas), became dominant in Rationalism (cf. Descartes, Malebranche, Leibniz, etc.), only to be critiqued by Kant, for whom such argumentation underlies any type of proof for divine existence. In the 20th Century (cf. Herman Malcolm) the argument has been revised and creatively developed. The ensuing study will examine the specific version of this argument used by Josiah Royce, a version that received the praise of William James. This study will focus solely on the young Royce's argumentation (ca. 1892) and reconstruct the argument in terms of Royce's idealistic pre-suppositions. The argument presented is not so much an attempt to "prove" definitively divine existence (though the author considers the argument to be valid) as it is an effort to be provocative, hopefully eliciting contrary opinions. Further examination of Anselmian logic is certainly to be desired.

Key-words: Proof of divine existence, ontological argument,
Realism, Idealism, Josiah Royce

I. Declaration of Thematic Intent

Responding to the monk Gaunilon, his first major critic, St. Anselm of Canterbury (AD 1033/34-1109), proffers perhaps inadvertently a definition of God which is surprising or, at least, has a particularly Anselmian flare: "God . . . is that about which nothing greater can be thought"[1] To all intents and purposes, a "concept" (or, as the one or the other apologist maintains, an "idea"[2]) appears to be predicated of God, thereby revealing something fundamentally pertinent to the divine essence. Yet, this so-called definition seems somewhat odd. The peculiarity of St. Anselm's definitional approach will manifest itself all the more clearly by comparing it with that of Spinoza.

Spinoza formulates his conceptualization of God in the following manner: "By God I understand an absolutely infinite being [*ens absolute infinitum*], that is, a substance consisting of infinite attributes, etc."[3] Spinoza does not consider the essence of God to be a function of the very act of "thinking" itself: The attributes postulated by Spinoza possess a content which is conceptually distinct from the act of thinking of these very attributes. Moreover, infinity itself is conceived of as the attribute par excellence. In contrast, one notable aspect of the Anselmian definition consists in the fact that thinking itself is part of the core of that which is thought about the divine essence. In other words, "thinking" forms the generative heart of the predication and is, at the same time, that which is being predicated. Be that as it may, Spinoza functions here only as a contrast. And that he is!

It should be stressed that the peculiarly Anselmian moment consists in the attempt to derive and to establish the very existence of God directly by means of this "mere" conceptualization, itself quite notable. According to St. Anselm, any attempt to deny such existence will conduct the thinker straight away into logical absurdities, i.e., he will be a "fool," an intellectual one, of course. Perhaps we have here the most shocking moment in the ontological argument[4]. Surely a certain audacity is being ascribed to the power of human thinking, indeed, an audacity itself curiously notable. Concerning such a philosophical novelty, Wolfgang Röd has written:

> The ontological argument, i.e. the intent to prove the existence of God solely on the basis of definitions and nominally on the basis of the definition of 'God? in accord with certain ontological axioms, is one of the most famous arguments in philosophy and perhaps the most notable [merkwürdig] one that has ever been undertaken. Equally notable is its history[5].

I propose to project myself into this "notable," indeed simply audacious, "history" by focusing upon the probative curiosity of such an "odd" argument. However, the following is of supreme importance for a correct understanding of my study:

I do not intend directly to prolong this history, however astute this story is, but rather to transform significantly the flow of this history in accord with my Roycean idealism. Readers should realize that I am in no direct way seeking to convince them of the validity of Anselm's "ontological argument". Ropero has insisted that "Anselm is a realist . . . and that there exists [for him] a universal absolute, namely God, the most really real.[6]" I suspect that whatever difficulties arise in the Anselmian argument probably result from any ontological realism in Anselm's thought. For this reason, strict fidelity to the thought of St. Anselm remains foreign to my project, which is to establish by the means of "thinking", of course, idealistically improved- the existence of God, the "most ideally ideal," expositing no more than aspects of such reasoning in Roycean terms. No doubt I will disfigure, seen materially, the Anselmian argument for the existence of God. Nevertheless, from a formal point of view, the ontological argument remains the fountain generating the ensuing reflection on the "Absolute" (the term preferred by Royce to designate God within a metaphysical context[7]).

II. The Role of Roycean Idealism

There are some specific reasons why I have selected Royce instead of, say, Bradley, Taylor, Bosanquet, Blanshard, Sprigge or others from the Anglo-American tradition of idealism, although from time to time one or the other will be cited. One reason is explicit and the other implicit. Let me pursue the matter:

First, Royce himself not only submitted the specific Anselmian argument to critical examination, but rather adopted what he considered to be the metaphysical heart of such a form of reasoning as his own "relational form of the ontological argument.[8]" Supposedly the weakness of the said mode of argumentation derives from the process of passing from essence to existence. Certainly, Kant deplored such a process, as did Royce's former student, George Santayana. According to Royce's opposing opinion: "Whoever says the evidence [i.e., the essential structure of something] shows the existence, holds that the essence gives some light on the existence.... Whoever appeals to evidence for existence is using some form of the ontological proof[9]" In other words, whatever data conceived as evidence for the existence of something, are equivalent to saying that said something exists. For example:

> Defining the past and the future in terms of their relation to the present, the essence of that relation, together with the datum of the present, is declared to warrant the assertion of the past existence of the past and the future existence. Granting the relation of the past and the future to the present, the essence of that relation in view of the present requires that

there shall have been a past and that there will be a future. ... Every reasoning on the basis of evidence to something not supposed to be a datum is a use of the ontological proof.[10]"

In other words, the present as the "right now" shows structurally and necessarily the existence of the past and of the future (which are not given as existent in that very "now"). It follows that time evinces a triadic structure which determines the necessary existence of this very structure. Resuming, Royce argues, in accord with the letter and the spirit of his idealism, along the lines of Anselm's ontological reasoning, I hold that it is worthwhile to reconsider freely the mode of thinking used by Anselm and reconstituted by Royce.

Second, some nineteen years before his explicit elaboration of the relational form of the ontological argument, Royce implicitly applied this very argumentative line in his provocative book on the conception of God[11]. Royce begins his discussion with a nominal idea respecting God, an idea probably acceptable even to the "fool":

> I propose to define, in advance, what we mean under the name "God," by means of using what tradition would call one of the Divine Attributes. I refer here to what has been called the attribute of Omniscience, or of the Divine Wisdom. By the word "God" I shall mean, a being who is conceived as possessing in the full all logically possible knowledge, insight, wisdom. Our problem, then, becomes at once this: Does there demonstrably exist an Omniscient Being? or is the conception of an Omniscient Being, for all that we can say, a bare ideal of the human mind?[12]

The concluding question is, without doubt, equally valid for the Anselmian conception of God. By means of a detailed examination of such a conception (divine essence) Royce believed to be able to demonstrate the existence of God. There is a similarity between the methodologies of Royce and Anselm. Both begin with an idea in order to proceed to the existence of God. Certainly all this prompts reflection; precisely this reflection will be pursued in the rest of my study.

Because of so many attacks and defenses of the ontological argument, Röd suspects (in reality he knows quite well) that: "the differences between defenders and opponents reside in silent presuppositions, i.e., in presupposed ontological axioms".[13] This is certainly valid in the case of Royce (and for this author). It is, consequently, of value to present and to examine just such "presuppositions," thereby hopefully justifying Royce's methodology of commencing with the divine essence in order to arrive at the affirmation of divine existence.

III. Presuppositions to a Roycean Evaluation of the Anselm's Argument

An understanding of Royce's idealism (and, for that matter, of Anglo-American idealism in general) can be, perhaps, best realized by distinguishing realism from idealism. In order to affect such an encounter, I shall cite a number of opinions, albeit selected and limited, concerning the essence of metaphysical realism:

Köhler: (1) There is something called the "world" or "reality" which exists *independently* [emphasis added] of the mind, of thought, of knowledge or of the language of human beings. ...
(2) That which is, is of a certain construction. ...
(3) The structures of reality are knowable. ...

Lelande: [Realism is] the doctrine according to which being is *independent* [emphasis added] of any actual cognizance which conscious subjects can take of it; *esse* is not the equivalent to *percipi*, even in the broadest sense that one can give to the word.

Ferrater Mora: Metaphysical realism affirms that things exist outside or *independently* [emphasis added] of the subject's consciousness.

Hirth: In modern philosophy, however, [realism] is used for the view that material objects exist externally to us and *independently* [emphasis added] of our sense experience.

Gredt Hac obiecta cognitionis obiiciuntur seu obtruduntur *independenter* [emphasis added] ab ipsa cognitione. ("These objects of cognition reveal and manifest themselves independently of cognition itself")

Sigwart: Whatever "is," it is not merely produced by my thought activity, rather is *independent* [emphasis added] of it, and remains [as it is], whether it is represented or not in any [given] moment.

Millán-Puelles: Question: Is not this indentation out of place? By 'realism' is meant that doctrine according to which the object of knowledge (of true knowledge, that is) constitutes authentic realities viz., beings capable of subsistence *independently* [emphasis added] of the knowledge.

Taylor: By Realism is meant the doctrine that the fundamental character of that which really is ... to be found in its *independence* [emphasis added] of all relation to the experience to a subject. What exists at all, the realist holds, exists equally whether it is experienced or not.[14].

Over and over there appears and reappears in the above somewhat monotonous definitions the same essential designation of the essence of realism: that which constitutes the reality of something is its *independence* of *all* consciousness[15]. Royce himself has proposed a similar conclusion:

> [Realism] asserts that just this independence of your knowing processes, of all such knowing processes, ... is not only a universal character of real objects, but also constitutes the very definition of the reality of the known object itself[16].

> According to this conception, I repeat, to be real means to be independent of an idea or experience through which the real being is, from without, felt, or thought, or known. And this, I say, is the view best known as metaphysical Realism.[17]

Evincing a striking misconception, Millán-Puelles, himself a Thomist realist, avers that for idealism the "object of knowing" is "merely ideal" and "without any teal correlative"[18]. If there is no reality correlative to ideas, then the demoralizing thesis of Millán-Puelles holds, namely that no judgment is possible concerning that which could be beyond the confines of finite human consciousness. We have here a contortion if not a perversion of idealism. If idealists thought as Millán-Puelles suggests, no discussion on the part of a realist (who well knows through his immediate self-experience that he is beyond the knowledge of the idealist) with an idealist would be possible because said idealist, *volens-nolens*, suffers truly from a serious mental problem. But, is it so that the idealist, by means of his judgments, refers to nothing beyond the fragments in his mind? One quotation from Royce should suffice to illustrate the falsity of the conception of Millán-Puelles (and of a number of other like-minded thinkers).

> We must not only seek Being as our [cognitive] goal, but we must correspond to its real constitution if we are to get the truth. And somehow it has that constitution. We have to submit. The Real may not be wholly independent of our thinking, but it is at least authoritative. [19]

Did Royce just adopt here a realist posture? No! The decisive formulation is "not wholly independent of our thinking [viz., consciousness]. Without a doubt, according to Royce, there are things, indeed, a whole world of things, beyond his own particular consciousness--itself quite *finite*. Following Royce, I add: Personally, I can represent to myself the market where just some hours ago I bought ice-cream for consumption this evening. More is possible: I can envision, using in part images seen in books and in television, the moon. Even more: I can imagine other planets, universes and even galaxies without limit. But what I cannot do in any way whatsoever (visually or logically) is represent a universe (or a simple market)

beyond all consciousness. Things beyond my consciousness? Yes! Beyond consciousness *per se*? No! If there is "reality" beyond my consciousness - my consciousness being here a representative of finite consciousness in itself - either I
can have no consciousness of such a state of affairs (and for this reason said
"thing'"' becomes semantic nonsense) or I represent an all-encompassing consciousness to which this world "beyond" appears. Still more: If I try to represent
any world without correlative consciousness, this said "world" beyond consciousness disappears in the very act of representing it, all of which is to say that there
was no act in the first place. A world beyond all experience, viz., consciousness, is
a meaningless construct. A *flatus vocis*, without doubt!

F. H. Bradley, an important inspiration for Royce, clearly manifests the idealist
thesis which I am seeking to use in a reconstruction of the ontological argument
of St Anselm:

> Find any piece of existence, take up anything that anyone could possibly
> call a fact, or could in any sense assert to have being, and then judge if it
> does not consist in sentient experience. Try to discover any sense in which
> you can still continue to speak of it, when all perception and feeling have
> been removed; or point out any fragment of its matter, any aspect of its
> being, which is not derived from and is not still relative to this source.
> When the experiment is made strictly, I can myself conceive of nothing else
> than the experience. Anything, in no sense felt or perceived, becomes to
> me quite meaningless.[20]

The Austrian idealist Reininger announces his idealism in a challenge to the realist:

> For us there is no Being which is not at the same time conscious Being
> [bewusstes Sein]. It immediately follows that no affirmation about the
> purely and simply non-conscious [*das schlechthin Unbewusste*] would be
> possible, even in the form of the recognition that "things are such.". . . Let
> anyone attempt to direct his thought at something non-conscious [*Nicht-
> Bewusstes*]! I could not know anything about something in no way present
> to consciousness [*von einem auf keiner Weise Bewussten*], I could not even
> say that I know nothing about the matter. Consciousness [*Bewusstheit*] . .
> . is an absolutely essential characteristic, the *indelibilis* characteristic of
> everything that can be the object of our reflections.[21]

Royce places himself effectively in accord with the theses of Bradley and Reininger, averting that:

> the beyond is itself content of an actual experience, the experience to be-
> yond is presented being in such intimate relation to the experience which

asserts the possibility, that both must be viewed as aspects of one whole, fragments of one organization.[22]

Do I have a reader who would like to respond to the challenge of Reininger and refute the theses of Bradley and Royce? If so, the readers not in agreement can realize such a task quite simply. Let him but direct his attention to any note, let us say a spot of green in front of his eyes, and then describe it (or simply point at it) in total absence of consciousness, including his own! Surely green not seen by anyone is, well, green, eternally green and that is all. Wrong! There is more! I suggest one more time that reader identifies and describes any mark of green, and that he then repress completely and most rigorously his (correlative) consciousness of said green mark. What remains after such a repression? First, with respect to the concrete color in question? Nothing, nothing and even more nothing! Second, in respect to himself, viz., to his consciousness? This nothingness is so ubiquitous, as Reininger noted, my reader in this concrete case would have no consciousness of having no consciousness of said green. In other words, he cannot recognize this situation because, by hypothesis, he has no awareness of it, i.e., neither of the content nor of the non-consciousness of this content. At any rate, not only does the specific green mark constitute nothing beyond experience, but also the one who has no experience of said mark is nothing. And nothing is, well, nothing! I, on the other hand, do possess consciousness of all this. I can describe in detail reality beyond my finite consciousness, but only on the "presupposition" that said content is present to an all-encompassing (super)consciousness of both it and of me. Royce resumes this thesis writing that:

> the reality that we seek to know has always to be defined as that which either is or would be present to a sort of experience which we ideally define as an organized . . . experience. We have, in point of fact, no conception of reality capable of definition except this one.[23]

If no one can communicate to me anything about that of which he has no consciousness, it seems to me that I am right, i.e., my thesis holds. The refutation of the idealistic argument appears to be so simple. Alas, semantically it is, sad to say, nonsense. It lacks any sense, it is senseless. Are we all of one mind on this point? If there is consensus, are we not all idealists? May my reader ponder it very well! This is not theatrics rather a challenge calling for reflection.

Résumé: Given the fact that realism is generally assumed as so obvious that even to reflect on the matter seems superfluous, I am well aware of the striking nature of my contentions up to this point. (To those readers who feel that my point of view is quite bizarre, I recommend that they familiarize themselves with the intellectual exchange between Royce and his former student, George Santayana, about a century ago - an illuminating battle of the minds[24].) Be that as it may, I have sought above to present a central thesis of idealism, namely the intrinsic and correlative connection between consciousness in general and the content present to it. Presuming that I have succeeded in my expository efforts, I will now begin my reconstruction of the ontological argument in the terms of Josiah Royce. |

IV. Roycean Meditations on the Ontological Argument

Heinrich Schmidinger informs us: "The proof of Anselm is justified or not in accord with the offered concept of God. It reads: aliquid quo maius nihil cogitari potest...[25] I shall let Emanuela Sctibano present a concise continuation of this line of argument:

(1) God is the Being about which nothing greater can be thought.
(2) A Being which exists both in the intellect as well as in reality is greater than mere being that exists only in the intellect.
(3) If God exists in the intellect, God exists also in reality.
(4) God is in the intellect.
(5) God is, therefore, in reality."

It seems to me (as it has to others) that, as in every theoretical argument, the validity of the conclusion, even if the argument is logically unflawed, depends upon the sustainability-of the premises. For us moderns (or worse, postmoderns), the concept of "'greater" is not above suspicion. This has certainly been seen as a weakness in the apparent logical solidity of Anselm's version of the ontological argument. For the moment, such scruples do not concern me.

Above I confessed that I have no intention to defend directly the Anselmian argumentation. I simply wish to utilize the methodology of such an argument in its Roycean form in order to submerge my philosophical curiosity in a search more than abstract for divine existence accessible to human reason. My mentor in this search has been Royce and his own form of the ontological argument For Royce, reflections about the omniscience of God (and certainly omniscience is *aliquid quo maius nihil no cogitari potest)* constitute much more than a mere intellectual pastime.

If it is worthwhile even to speak of God before the forum of the philosophical reason, it is so because one hopes to be able, in a measure, to translate into articulate terms the central mystery of our existence, and to get some notion about what is at the heart of the world.[27]

And the path leading to a partial comprehension of this central mystery consisted for Royce in the methodology of the ontological argument, whose point of departure is the conceptualization of the Divine Being. Royce differs here from Anselm in that the point of departure is not *quo maius nihil cogitari potest*, but rather divine omniscience - an insignificant difference in reality since both positions effectively presuppose the infinity of God, a quite common predicate ascribed to God.[28] Interestingly, Royce utilized a conceptualization of God which is purported to stem from St. Thomas, certainly no idealist.

> But the conception of the Divine that St. Thomas reached remains in certain important respects central, and in essence identical, I think, with 'the definition that I have tried to repeat... . I am certainly disposed to insist that what the faith of our fathers has genuinely meant by God is, despite all the blindness and the unessential accidents of religious tradition, identical with the inevitable outcome of reflective philosophy.[29]

What a paradox! An ontological argument of idealist nature that begins with a Thomist premise! Well, the moment for argumentative reflection has arrived!

The reasoning: Every thinker, even the "fool,'" accepts, at least provisionally in the case of atheists, the attribute of omniscience as pertinent to the definition of Divine Being. No?[30] How can a finite thinker represent Omniscient Being?

> An Omniscient Being would be one who simply found present to him, not by virtue of fragmentary and gradually completed processes of inquiry, but by virtue of an all-embracing, direct, and transparent insight into his own truth - who found thus present to him, I say, the complete, the fulfilled answer to ever genuinely rational question.[31]

For this reason, Royce maintains that the "Omniscient Being . . . would possess what we may call an Absolute Thought . . . [and] that the experience and thought of this being might be called completely or fully organized,[32] (And by the term "experience" Royce refers to consciousness.) Simply put, it is a matter of an "Absolute Consciousness." Such a thesis is but a necessary implication proceeding from the original predication.

Doubtless such a thesis by Royce provokes an important response in the form of a question: Does there really exist such an Omniscient Being or is such a conceptualization nothing but a soothing ideal for a finite consciousness that is a prisoner of *Sorge* (Heidegger)? Is it possible rationally to establish the existence of such a Sublime Being merely by means of a mere conceptualization? Or is it, perhaps, since God remains hidden from direct rational insight, that at best only indirect ways (e. g., the Thomist proofs not particularly convincing in the days of Royce) could be adduced to "prove" the existence of a God so removed from any immediate comprehension? In Royce's opinion (naturally in accord with his idealistic presuppositions), as in the case of St. Anselm, it is truly possible to commence a proof of divine existence based upon an intellectual "'vision" of divine essence.

For both Royce and Anselm, the price of negating such a vision leads the doubting thinker into the "foolish" realm of self-contradiction, a realm that could lead one into a sort of insanity[33] .At this point, let us pursue the various stages of Royce's (effectively) ontological argument.

(1) First of all, let us commence with a question: What do we have at our disposition if we render a true (or false) judgment? In the case of truth-possession we have "true ideas, fulfilled, confirmed, verified by your experiences,[34]" such truths being valid for all times. In other words, belief that a proposition is true means that we comprehend it as being confirmed, certified or verified from a point of view transcending the totality of the finite experience of each and every human judgment, distributively or collectively. This entails, then, presence to an all-encompassing "vision" capturing the universality of a given truth. Repress this all-encompassing vision, and we have no truth that transcends the moment and place of its being asserted. The same holds for falsity

> To conceive any human belief as false - say, the belief of a lunatic, a fanatic, a philosopher, or a theologian - is to conceive this opinion as either possibly or actually corrected from some higher point of view, to which a larger whole of experience is considered as present.[35]

In short, the human obtainment of truth or falsity structurally entails a certain form, viz., certain components and their (inter-)relation as given to the mind (or consciousness) that judges. In other words: (a) there is the moment of the act of judging, (b) that which is so or so judged, and (c) the vision (i.e., consciousness) of the coincidence (correspondence) or not of judgment and judged. Because of human finitude it is always possible to separate "the unity of thought and fact, the illumination of feeling by comprehension"[36] into its component parts. Up to this point I have separated out the component of experience (i.e., consciousness) and hopefully thematized it adequately. The next question concerns the very content of reality in itself in contrast to its presentation to or in consciousness,

(2) That which constitutes the material manifold of the contents of reality is surely of enormous interest to our concrete lives. However, in the context of my discussion this vanity is only of interest relative to its *formality*. Above I sought to show that reality does not consist, neither formally nor materially, in being beyond all experience or, rather, consciousness. That which is beyond all consciousness is, without further ado, nothing more than "nothing"! Not even a "cosmic materialism" with its physical, indeed, transcendental beyond can escape universal consciousness.[37] I believe we can safely say that "reality" in and by its formality is that which appears to awareness, i.e., must be considered relative to content as the material component presenting itself, formally speaking, to an experience (or consciousness), though often such content exists beyond the finite consciousness of

humans but not beyond consciousness in and by itself, Without experience in and of itself there is no reality of which a thinker can even conceive, i.e., there exists nothing more than the nothingness about which Reininger noted so much above. All this being granted, Royce designates the realm correlative to Absolute Experience as "Absolute Reality"[38] Royce explains:

> That which man being intrinsically finite[39] now lacks, in so far as he is ignorant of the Absolute Reality, is logically definable as a possible, but to us unattainable, sort of experience; namely, precisely an experience of what reality is.[40]

Only in the terms of an Absolute Experience (or Absolute Consciousness) is it possible to claim truth validity for a thesis, if the validity of this thesis is to transcend the concrete here and now of the assertion. In other words, a truth, universally valid for all times and places (and it is such or it is not verity), pertains, formally *presented*, to a "beyond" each and every finite consciousness. Above I imagined the market of this morning, not to speak of the moon and universes without limit. Such "realities" obtain their *veritable meaning* only as the material contents correlative to an Absolute Experience. Summarizing, Royce proclaims: "'And by reality we mean merely the contents that would be present to such an ideal unity of experience". [41]

(3) The Moment of Truth (or, alas, falsity): Royce, departing from his reference to omniscience as a nominal definition of God, seeks to derive from this omniscience God's necessary existence. Furthermore, basing his argument on the principle of the correlation between absolute reality and absolute experience, he analytically examines the components of experience in order to lead the foolish doubter to the certain existence of an Omniscient God. We have just followed Royce along his chosen path of argumentation. Nevertheless, are matters really so? Well then, let us bow to the skeptic and presume that matters are not really so. Perhaps there is no necessity that omniscient experience should be, viz., exist? Perhaps. It seems wise to attempt such a doubt.

> Grant hypothetically, if you choose, for a moment, that there is no universal experience as a concrete fact, but only the hope of it, the definition of it, the will to win it . . . in the error of believing that it is. Well, what will that mean?[42]

The response must be demoralizing for a thinker who might wish to possess a rationally solid foundation for his faith. Instead of blessed possession, such a thinker, such a doubter, finds his conscious efforts forced to affirm that finitude is the fruition of his rational search for God. This seems to imply that God remains in some way hidden from reason (or, worse, does not exist). Royce continues on his argumentative path contending that this absolute finiteness and erroneousness of the real experience, I say, will itself be a fact, a truth, a reality, and, as such, just the absolute truth. But this supposed ultimate truth will exist for whose experience [viz., consciousness]? For the finite experience?[43]

By means of such tantalizing queries we arrive at the very perplexing heart of the analysis. Royce answers his own questions responding:

> No, for although our finite experience knows itself to be limited, still, just in so far as it is finite, it cannot know that there is no unity beyond its fragmentariness [i.e., finitude]. For if any experience actually knew (that is, actually experienced) itself to be the whole of experience, it would have to experience how and why it were so. And if it knew this, it would be ipso facto an absolute, i.e., a completely self-possessed, experience, for which there was no truth that was not, as such, a datum, . . . no thought to which a presentation did not correspond, no presentation whose reality was not luminous to its comprehending thought. Only such an absolute experience could say with assurance: "Beyond my world there is no further experience actual."[44]

It is exactly at this point that the onto-semantic problem begins. "For truth is, in so far as it is known [present to consciousness]."[45] This thesis is just a summary of Royce's argument as already developed. At any rate, Royce concludes immediately:

> Now this proposition applies as well to the totality of the world of finite experience as it does to the parts of that world. There must, then, be an experience to which is present the constitution (Le, the actual limitation and narrowness) of all finite experience, just as surely as there is such a constitution. That there is nothing at all beyond this limited constitution must, as a fact, be present to this final experience.[46]

A denial of such a final experience is simply impossible because such a denial leads the thinker into a contradiction, an auto-contradiction. Why?

> But this fact that the world of finite experience has no experience beyond it could not be present, as a fact, to any but an absolute experience which knew all that is or that genuinely can be known; and the proposition that a totality of finite experience could exist without any absolute experience, thus proves to be simply self-contradictory.[47]

Self-contradiction arises: here because, applying Royce's presupposition of the necessary correlation between content and experience (viz., consciousness),

whatever "beyond" consciousness (be this "beyond" something or pure nothing[ness]) postulated as fully independent of all consciousness (not just human
awareness) contradicts the very conditions presupposed for the very onto-semantic possibility of the proposition itself, i.e., namely, a context of existence and consciousness as constitutive of truth assertion. A fully all-encompassing consciousness is quite necessary for any truth, even the supposed truth that there is no such
consciousness (which, in turn, will "seem" as false in or to a said all-encompassing
awareness). "The very effort to deny an absolute experience involves, then, the
actual assertion of such an absolute experience.[48] The very ontological possibility
of truth necessarily entails a final experience in which, and for which, this truth is.

Now, in the terminology of Royce's argument, such a "final experience" is just
another name for God, i.e., "a being who is conceived as possessing to the full all
logically possible knowledge, insight, wisdom.[49] What began as a definition, as a
statement of essence, has now been shown, based upon Royce's idealistic premises, to be not only "a bare ideal of the human mind",[50] but rather an ultimate
existence. Royce has, in the spirit of his relational form of the ontological argument, departed from essence in order to arrive at existence. The very denial of
the existence of "all logically possible knowledge, insight, wisdom," presupposes
for its very own existence a final and absolute (i.e., without limits) truth for final
and absolute consciousness. *Quod erat demonstrandum!*

In my judgment, if Royce is to be refuted then it can only be on the basis of his
idealistic presuppositions. I see no broken logical link in the persuasive dialectic
pursued by Royce, which I have exposed here. If "falsity" is to be established,
then it must be found in the premises of the relational form of the ontological
argument, not in the logic of the argument itself presented above.

Final word: I should like to give finality to my exposition by noting an evaluation
of Royce offered by his contemporary, George Holmes Howison, who seemed to
believe that Royce was a pantheist - a critique which Royce rejected. John
Clendenning in his charming biography of Royce recounts the perplexity felt by
Howison:

> Why, Howison asked, was Royce unwilling to remain a sceptic? Why must
> the absolute save us from endless contradiction? The answer, Howison be-
> lieved, lay in the strategy of the argument. It was Royce's method to apply
> "'a clinching dialectical thumbscrew for the torture of agnostics." Speaking
> to the unbeliever, but not to the believer, Royce was in effect saying: Your
> doubts are doomed, for either you must surrender the grounds that make
> doubt possible or you must admit that your doubts are included in an ab-
> solute truth.[51]

The same strategy mentioned by Howison has configured the development of my Roycean argument, but with one difference! The object of my method has been of more universal concern: that is, in place of the agnostic I have applied "a clinching dialectical thumbscrew" to the theoretical torture of realists, be they agnostic, atheists or even believers. The purification enacted by my argumentative conjurations has followed my desire to exorcise from theological thought the realist's doctrine of (absolute) independence of reality beyond all consciousness. I certainly would appreciate any attempt to refute the argument given above, because the world of contemporary idealists does not evince a plethora of company. Or, perhaps, my reader might possibly wish to join me on my island of the idealistic Robinson Crusoe. Reservations are now being accepted!

Footnotes

† All translations into English in the following analysis are my own.

1   Anselm of Canterbury, "Quid Ad Haec Respondeat," adjunct to *Proslogion* (Pamplona: Eunsa, 2002), I.

2   Alfonso Ropero, *Introducción a la filosofia*: *Su historia en relación con la teología*, 3rd ed. (*Barcelona*: Editorial CITE, 1999), 214.

3   Spinoza, *Ethica*, I. def. 6.

4   For bibliographies on Anselm, cf. Pérez de Laborda and Luis Pablo Turin, "Introduction, Translation and notes," in *St. Anselmo, Prosiogion* (Pamplona: Eunsa, 2002);

     Eudaldo Forment, *Anselmo (1033/34—-1109)* (Madrid: Ediciones del Otro, 1995), 90-94;

     Robert Theis, ed., *Anselm von Canterbury, Proslogion, Anrede.* (Latein/Deutsch) Stuttgart Reclam, 2005), 127—31;

     Rogelio Roviera, *La fuga del no ser: El argumento ontológica de la existencia de Dios y los problemas de la metafísica* (Madrid: Encuentro, 1991), 205-7.

     There are innumerable discussions of Anselm in histories of philosophy. However, most are superficial and, hence, will not be noted here.

5   Wolfgang Röd, *Der Gott der reinen Vernunft: Die Auseinandersetzung um den ontologischen Gottesbeweis von Anselm bis Hegel* (München:. Beck, 1992), 13.

6   Ropero, *Introducción a la filosofía*, 211.

7   Cf. Josiah Royce, *The Problem of Christianity* (Chicago; University of Chicago Press, 1968). In this book, published posthumously, I believe Royce analyzed Christian doctrine for more than 400 pages without once mentioning the term "absolute." Such an absence has led some scholars to the opinion that Royce had abandoned his absolute idealism. That this was not so can readily be seen in his last lectures from 1915-16, recently published. See Footnote 8 immediately below.

8   Josiah Royce, *Metaphysics* (Albany: State University of New York Press, 1998), 115-42.

9   Ibid, 125.

10   Ibid., 131.

11   Cf. Josiah *Royce and* Others, The Conception of God: A Philosophical Dis-
        cussion *Concerning the Nature of the Divine Idea as a Demonstrable Reality*
        (New York: Mcmillian, 1898), 3-51.

12   Royce and others, *The Conception of God*, 7.

13   Röd, *Der Gott der reinen Vernunft*, 22.

14   Cf. Wolfgang R. Kohler, introduction (Einleitung) to *Realismus und Anti-Re-
        alismus*, (Frankfurt am Main, Suhrkamp, 1992), 7; André Lalande, Real-
        isme," in *Vocabulaire technique et critique de la philosophie* (Paris: Presses
        Universitaires de France, 1983), 892; *Diccionario de la filosofia* (Madrid:
        Alianza, 1986), s.v. "Realismo": *The Encyclopedia of Philosophy* (New York:
        Macmillan, 1967), s.v. "Realism": Josephus Gredt, *Elementa philosophae
        Aristotelico-Thomisticae*, 13th ed, (Barcelona: Herder, 1961), 1:81;Chris-
        toph von Sigwart, *Logik*, 2nd ed. (Tübingen, 1890), 1: 90; Antonio Millán-
        Puelles, *Léxico filosófico*, 2nd ed. (Madrid: Rialp, 2002), 351; Alfred Edward
        Taylor, *Elements of Metaphysics* (NewYork: University Paperbacks, 1903),
        67.

15   Literature about Royce is not exactly excessive. Nevertheless, John
        Clendenning has published an excellent bibliography of works on the life
        and thought of Royce. Cf. *The Life and Thought of Josiah Royce* (Vanderbilt
        Vanderbilt University Press, 1999), 420-26.

16   Josiah Royce, *The World and the Individual*, Vol. 1, *The Four Historical Con-
        ceptions of Being* (Gloucester, MA: Peter Smith, 1976), 66.

17   Ibid., 62.

18   Antonio Millán-Puelles, *Fundamentos de filosofía*, 12th ed. (Madrid: Rialp, 1985),
        467-68.

19   Royce, The *Four Historical Conceptions of Being*, 299.

20   Francis Herbert Bradley, *Appearance and Reality: A Metaphysical Essay*,
        2nd ed. (Oxford: Clarendon, 1978), 127-29. A. E. Taylor, himself an idealist,
        writes: "If we take the term 'actual' to denote that which is thus indissolu-
        ble from immediate apprehension ... [then] there is no possibility outside
        actual existence, and that statements about the possible . . . are always an
        indirect way of imparting information about actualities . . . [which] actually
        exist as part of the contents of an experience which is not our own," *Ele-
        ments of Metaphysics*, 26.

21 Robert Reininger, *Metaphysik der Wirklichkeit* (München: Reinhardt, 1970), 1; 23-24.

22 Royce and others, *The Conception of God*, 168.

23 Ibid.

24 In this context, Royce engaged in a critical polemic with Santayana, citing long quotations from Santayana for examination. Cf. *Metaphysics*, 93-142.

25 Heinrich Schmidinger, *Metaphysik: Ein Grundkurs* (Stuttgart: Kohlhammer, 2000), 129.

26 Cf. Emanuela Scribano, *L'existence de Dieu: Histoire a la preuve ontologique de Descartes à Kant* (Paris: Seuil, 2002), 39. For a further, quite critical, study of the ontological argument, cf. Simon L. Frank, *Der Gegenstand des Wissens: Grundlagen und Grenzen der begrifflichen Erkenntnis* (Freiburg; Alber, 2000, orginally 1915 in Russia). In 1921 Lenin offered Frank, then a professor at the University of Saint Petersburg, the choice of either migrating or remaining in Russia for execution. Frank's choice was as simple as it was obvious.

27 Royce and others, *The Conception of God*, 6.

28 Cf. Antonio Millán -Puelles, "Atributos Divinos Entiativos," in *Léxico Filosófico* (Madrid: Rialp, 1985), 53-54.

29 Royce and others, *The Conception of God*, 49-50.

30 Millán-Puelles provides an excellent example of the Thomistic inability to comprehend more than a truncated version of idealism. Cf. his article "Idealismo y realismo," in *Léxico Filosófico*, 348-57. Although Thomists hold that God possesses infinite consciousness, they do not consider this "fact" relevant to what idealism has to say on consciousness. It seems that in Thomism, consciousness is a fortunate accompaniment.

31 Royce and others, *The Conception of God*, 8.

32 Ibid., 14.

33 I am not trying to gain points with my thesis. The loss of 'reality, at least *psychologically* speaking, is an integral part of the "meaningless" viz., "empty" world of schizophrenia. Cf. Silvano Ariete, *Interpretation of Schizophrenia* (New York: Brunner, 1955), 83-173 and Ernest Becker, "Religion: The Quest for Ideal Heroism," in *The Birth and Death of Meaning: An* Interdisciplinary *Perspective on the Problem of Man*, 2nd ed. (New York: Free Press, 1971), 180-200. Becker elaborated his thesis in his magnum opus,

The Denial of Death (New York: Free Press, 1973), especially 255-85. So the "fool" to whom Anselm referred is quite possibly a person in danger.

34 Royce and others, *The Conception of God*, 9. 7

35 Ibid., 31.

36 Ibid., 12.

37 CL Gustavo Bueno with his "cosmic materialism" in which terms such as "transcendental Materiality"' pop up in *Materia* (Oviedo: Pentalfa, 1990), 48-50.

38 Royce and others, *The Conception of God*, 19.

39 In his first major book Royce frequently used the term "infinity", much more than in *The* Conception *of God*. Cf. Royce, *The Religious Aspect of Philosophy: A Critique of the Bases of Conduct and of Faith* (New York: Harpers, 1958). Royce's first "proof" for divine: existence, viz., for the Absolute, is found in this study, cf. 384-426, This proof derives from a consideration of the nature of truth, a consideration I will soon take up again for another examination of divine reality. Royce's book did not constitute a dry discussion about Infinite Consciousness, but rather manifests a disquieting awareness of the problem of evil in terms of a Good God. Royce's attitude was, I believe, somewhat typical of American intellectuals at the turn of the 20th Century who contemplated the social plight at the end of, what Royce dubbed, "tough individualism." Royce's concern for social problems probably dates from his childhood days in California (1855ff.), the "gold rush days." Certainly he witnessed much avarice, criminality and mistreatment (and also a marginalization of the Mexican inhabitants). Cf. Royce, *California from the Conquest in 1846 to the Second Vigilance Committee in San Francisco: A Study of American Character* (Boston: Houghton Mifflin, 1886). Suffering and malevolence affected Royce profoundly. (Politically, he could be viewed as a forerunner to the supporters of the program of Social Security.) At any rate, beginning in 1878 Royce, as one of the first Californians, taught at the University of California at Berkeley - the university where my own mother, not born all too far from the Royce's place of birth, was one of the first female students at the university, majoring in mathematics and Latin. Personally, I have always sensed something of California in the thought of Royce, perhaps because I too am a son of that territory.

40 Royce and others, *The Conception of God*, 19.

41 Ibid., 35.

42   Ibid., 39.

43   Ibid.,40.

44   Ibid.

45   Ibid.

46   Ibid., 41.

47   Ibid.

48   Ibid., 43.

49   Ibid., 7.

50   Ibid.

51   Cf. John Clendenning, *The Life and Thought of Josiah Royce* (Vanderbilt: Vanderbilt Univ. Press, 1999), 203.

Bibliography

Anslem of Cantebury. *Proslogion*. Pamplona: Eunsa, 2002.

Ariete, Silvano. *Interpretation of Schizophrenia*. New York: Brunner, 1955.

Becker, Ernest. "Religions: The Quest for Idea Heroism", in *The Birth and Death of Meaning: An Inter-Disciplinary Perspective on the Problem of Man*. New York: Free Press, 1971. Pp. 180-200.

_____ . *The Denial of Death*. New York: Free Press, 1975.

Bradley, Francis Herbert. *Appearance and Reality: A Metaphysical Essay*. 2nd Edition. Oxford: Clarendon, 1978.

Bueno, Gustavo. *Matria*. Oviedo: Pentalfa, 1990.

Clendenning, John. *The Life and Thought of Josiah Royce*. Vanderbilt: Vanderbilt Universty Press, 1999.

Ferrater Mora, José. *Diccionario de la filosófia*. Vol. IV Q-Z. Madrid: Alianza, 1986.

Forment, Eudaldo. *Anselmo (1033/34-1109)*. Madrid: Ediciones del Otro, 1995.

Frank, Simon L. *Der Gegenstand des Wissens. Grundlagen und Grenzen der begrifflichen Erkenntnis*. Freiburg: Alber, 2000.

Gredt, Josephus. *Elementa philosophae Aristotelico-Thomisticae*-Barcerlona: Hereder, 1961.

Hirth, J. S. "Realism" in *The Encyclopedia of Philosophy*. Edited by Donald Bochert, 7:77. New York: Macnillan, 1967.

Köhler, Wolfgang R., Editor. *Realismus und Anti-Realismus*. Frankfurt: Surkamp, 1992.

Laborda, Pérez de, and Luis Pablo Turín. *St. Anselmo, Proslogion*. Pamplona: Eunsa, 2002.

Lalande, André. *Vocabulaire, technique et critique de la philosophie*. Paris: Presses Universitaires de France, 1983 (originally 1926)

Millán-Puelles, Antonio. *Fundamentos de filosófia*. 12th ed. Madrid Rialp, 1985.

_____ . *Léxico filosófico*, 2nd ed. Madrid: Rialp, 2002

Reininger, Robert. *Metaphysik der Wirklichkeit*. München: Reinhardt, 1970.

Ropero, Alonso. *Introducción a la filosófia: Su historia en relación con la teologia*. 3rd ed. Barcelona: Editorial CIIE, 1999.

Roviera, Regelio. *La fuga de no ser: El argumento ontológico de la existencia de Dios.* Madrid: Encuentro, 1991

Royce, Josiah. *California from the Conquest of 1846 to the Second Vigilance Committee in San Francisco. A Study in American Character* (1886). Boston Houghton, Miffin, 1889.

_____ . *Metaphysics.* Edited by William Ernest Hocking, Richard Hocking and Frank Oppenheim. New York: State University Press. 1998.

_____ . The *Problem of Christianity.* Chicago: University of Chicago Press, 1968.

_____ . *The Religious Aspect of Philosophy.* New York: Harpers, 1955.

_____ . *The World and the Individual.* First Series.: *Four Historical Concepts of Being*, MA: Peter Smith, 1976.

Royce, Josiah and Joseph le Conte, G H. Howison, and Sidney Edward Mezes. *The Conception of God: A Philosophical Historical Discussion Concerning the Nature of the Divine Ideas as a Demonstrable Reality.* New York: Macmillan, 1898.

Röd, Wolfgang. *Der Gott der reinen Vernunft Die Auseinandersetzung um den ontologischen Gottesbeweis von Anselm bis Hegel.* München: Beck, 1992.

Schmidinger, Heinrich. *Metaphysik: Ein Grundkurs.* Stuttgart: Kohlhammer, 2000.

Epilogue:

Addendum to the Ontological Argument

Preface: The article reprinted in Chapter 4 was originally written with an ironic tinge, boarding on divertive polemics, having the purpose to challenge my reader, if not to agree with my argument, then at least to take stock of the conceptual ingredients used in the attempted probative argument of an ontological nature. To be sure I only adduced one ontological argument, namely that of Josiah Royce, and then perhaps treated a bit too courtly. There are other versions and different lines of that argument, even in the case of Royce[1], though a common thread runs through most. Rhetorically, however, the logic of the argument served my polemical purposes of challenging my reader. In this short epilogue, I will not indulge in rhetorical flares, just focus upon what I take to be the broad structure of the conflict between realism and idealism as evidenced in the acceptance or rejection of the ontological argument. Royce forcefully posed his idealism in opposition to the realist claim that reality is what it *is qua* being fully *independent* of consciousness, viz., of being cognized. In this epilogue, I intend no more than to outline without rhetorical embellishment what I take to be the central nexus of the conflictive opposition entailed in any encounter between realism and idealism and why I hold that idealism prevails over realism. In this context, I shall rework Royce's argumentation by clearly revealing its presuppositions.

Realism: From the quotations on realism that I presented in the last chapter and from Royce's own understanding, it is clear that realism conceives that the cognitive situation entails two factors: namely, the existence of something "out there" *really* independent of the human mind, of human knowing, viz., a reality whose contents, whose very "being", constitute objectively separate entities complete in their own right, i.e., they retain their own essential properties *independent* of any cognitive relation that they might enter into. In other words, the cognitive relation of being-known by a knower, of being present to consciousness, is in no way a prerequisite for or determinant of the very being (*esse*) of the object, i.e., relative to either what something is or that it is. *Being-known is in no way a feature of being real in itself.* This feature is not something predicated to things, rather it constitutes *apriori* an indelible character of the thingness of things. Independence is not a causal relationship, rather a structural note of each reality. Realism as a metaphysical doctrine, thankfully, does not depend upon a materialist metaphysics[2]. It does entail, however, a basic ontological commitment to an ontological separation flowing necessarily from independence as the mark of reality of any object. The realist, Nicholas Rescher, states the central thesis of realism:

The ontological thesis is that there is a mind-independent physical reality to which our inquires address themselves more or less adequately—always imperfectly—is the key concept of realism. ... Our commitment to realism is, on this account, initially not a product of our inquiries about the world but rather reflects a facet of how we conceived the world[3].

C. I. Lewis (1883-1968), a cautious thinker, a former student of Royce and the founder of "conceptual pragmatism", effectively spells out the meaning of Rescher's words and thereby illustrates my thesis above:

In terms of experience and knowledge, the independence of reality—its independence of the knowing mind—means, first the *giveness* of what is given, our realization that we do not create this content of experience and cannot, by the activity of thinking, alter it. Second, it means that truth of those "if—then" propositions in which the process of possible experience, starting from the given, could be expressed. The "if" here depends upon our own active nature for its meaning, ... but the content of the "then" clause, and the truth of the propositions as a whole, are things with respect to which the knowing mind is not dictator but dictated to. ... But *what I should then find*; ... that is something independent of any purpose or attitude of mine. ... Third, the independence of reality means the transcendence by reality of our present knowledge of it. ... I know something in reality which is neither implicitly nor explicitly determined in my knowledge of it[4].

I take Lewis' assertion as a prototypical statement revealing the understanding of realism, although a statement that needs further consideration. Neither Lewis not Rescher, excluded idealism from being in some way valid. First, let us look at Rescher who writes of idealism

Idealism, broadly speaking, is the doctrine that reality is somehow mind correlative or mind coordinated. ... Idealism centers on the conception of reality as we understand it reflects the workings of the mind. And it construes this as meaning that the inquiring mind itself makes a formative contribution, not merely to our understanding of the nature of the real, but even to the resulting character we attribute to it (*SPI*, 304).

Rescher does not deny the function, nor the contribution of the mind in process of theoretical thinking about an object of interest. On the contrary, Rescher brilliantly illustrates what he meant in his early work on "conceptual idealism" wherein he notes:

Whenever and however we conceive of the particulars that constitute some sector of natural reality, we do so by means of the specific conceptualizing mechanisms that we ourselves bring to the *cognitive* situation.

The conceptual machinery—through its own nature-conditions—canalizes, and in some ways restricts how we represent things to ourselves in thought an d discourse. This has the consequence that ... the mind in part determines (i.e., significantly shapes and influences) the materials of knowledge. ...

Thus, the general position to be argued here might properly be characterized as *conceptual idealism*

...On this view what the mind 'makes' is not nature itself, but the mode-and-manner-determining categories in terms of which we conceive it[5].

... [R]eality is seen as the ontological *source* of cognitive endeavors, affording the existential matrix in which we move and have our being, and whose impact upon us is the prime movers for our cognitive efforts. All of these facets of the concept of reality are integrated and unified in the classical doctrine of truth as it corresponds to fact (*adequatio ad rem*), a doctrine that makes sense only in the setting of a commitment to mind-independent reality (*SPI*, 264).

I too hold to a basic correspondence theory of truth, its criterion being to a large degree a function of coherence[6]. I, the idealist, agree that, if there is no reality independent of the consciously judging *mind*, then correspondence truth is not possible, simply because there is nothing to correspond to. (Cf. Chapter 2 of this study on the being of truth.) So, I agree with the realist position that reality (= the arbitrator between "seeming" and "is") must imply *independence* from the *human* mind, no matter how much of the conceptuality of interpreting reality is derived from the rational categories generated by the human mind. If idealism and realism are understood as concepts *solely* derived from and referring *only* to the human *mind* (and that is Rescher's thesis as shown in his definitions), then realism would, indeed, be *the* key to the ontology of the world of reality, yet I remain ontologically an idealist. How so?

Idealism: Rescher can define idealism as he chooses, though the choice can be short sighted, even distorting. Rescher explicitly thinks that he was doing nothing but updating the thought of German Idealism by limiting the creative power of mental activity *per se* to being but a contributory factor of the *human* mind in the understanding of the world. The absolute mind of German idealism was reduced to the limits of the human mind *per se*. Rescher has had, to be sure, much "pragmatic" success with his limitation of idealism to the human *mind*, only, unfortunately, eliminating the ontological nature of idealism in the process, which certainly constitutes a falsification of the idealism entailed in Royce's ontological argument for God, viz., the Absolute, viz., an infinite consciousness. It is just such a consciousness (*Bewußtsein*) that I will outline when I turn to Robert Reininger's theorem of consciousness as the basis for an ontological idealism (including mine)[7].

One somewhat paradoxical origin of Royce's idealism can be gleaned from his reaction to the endless utterances of realists concerning independence, examples of which I supplemented in Chapter 4. Realism is so significant for understanding Royce and idealism because, all the while realists preach independence, they fail to notice that they never really say anything about things in their supposed strict independence, about what the thing is once removed from being present to the very same predicating consciousness uttering the thesis. What is a thing in itself in its full and total independence? The result is that the so-called independence of the things of the world *qua* being in the world, yet beyond consciousness, has no meaning, results in semantic vacuity. To be sure, the idealist does agree with the realist that the conscious human *mind* can well assert that there is reality beyond human knowing, i.e., from *being known* (by a mind), but not beyond consciousness *per se*. Rescher's limiting consciousness just to the human mind is not a true representation of ontological idealism, because the inexorable coincidence of being and consciousness in idealism is not between the human mind and the object of which said mind has consciousness. The connection is between anything that might be postulated as being (= *to be, esse, Sein*), constituting an *indissoluble* oneness between consciousness *per se* and being (*to be, esse, Sein*). Semantically, it is not possible to speak of reality, of reals, of "something" beyond consciousness *per se*, period! It is not even possible to be aware of not recognizing an object truly outside all consciousness as an "is". Such an indissoluble connection did not escape Reininger, indeed, he views the coincidence of being (*to be, Sein*) and consciousness (*Bewußtsein*) as necessary and sharing fully the same extensionality. Reininger writes:

> The very first prerequisite of every philosophy, behind which to go shows itself as simply impossible, is that something "is" at all. ... But only if a being exists not only *an sich* and for itself [= realism], but if it is also there "for me" [= idealism], can it become an object of my thought. To be there for me is to be conscious [bewußt]. Thus, only with conscious being can philosophy commence. ... The "to be there for me" [= consciousness] determines above all else the conceptual content of consciousness [Bewußtheit]. From that, there follows that ... the concepts of *to be* [*Sein*] and *consciousness* [*Bewußtsein*] coincide according to their extension.

That [fact] expresses the *principle of consciousness: There is for us no to be (or being) [Sein] that is not at the same time conscious being [bewußtes Sein]* (MW 20, 23-24).

(I must confess that my translation is not fully accurate, nor can it be because English cannot express accurately the German original.)

Wherever there are beings that *be*, they *are* present to consciousness *per se*. The meaning of Reininger's equation between whatever is (*Sein*) and consciousness (*Bewußtsein*) was effectively formalized in a parallel manner by the British idealist F. H. Bradley. Richard Wollheim, of analytical proclivities, ordered, and then criticized Bradley's argumentation. I will now cite Wollheim who separates Bradley's contention into four different sections for logical analysis—and I ask the reader to understand "consciousness" every time Wollheim refers to "experience":

Everything that we come across or accept as real, everything that we call a piece of existence or a fact, is always found *combined* with experience;

and it is always *combined with experience*, then no meaning can be attached to the assertion that it could exist without experience;

and if it could not exist without experience, then it is indivisible from experience;

and if it is indivisible from experience, then it is, or is nothing but, experience (Italics added)[8].

It is to be noted that Wollheim begins the recapitulation of Bradley's argument using the term "combined with", which semantically suggests that the *combined* elements (= object known and the knowing subject are merely or accidentally juxtaposed, hence separable and independent of each other. Being *merely* combined with experience was and is not Bradley's position, hence Wohlheim falsifies his reconstruction of Bradley's argument. Given the reconstruction, Wollheim agrees with the first thesis, but rejects any necessary connection—and logically so based on his misconstruction. Wollheim, in a truly analytic manner, explains Bradley's error noting that Bradley used "imaginable" in an ambiguous manner, claiming that Bradley's imagining an object was no more than merely to postulate it, but "not to make it an object of experience" (*FHB*, 203). Further, argues Wollheim, an event can be imagined, viz., postulated that is not being experienced; hence, logically, things can exist that are not experienced, i.e., not "combined" with consciousness. In truth, according to Wollheim, Bradley's contention (and derivatively Reininger's) "really establishes no more than that Everything is experience that is experienced" (*FHB*, 203). This, of course, is a tautology, self-deception, and nothing more, which has elicited a well-reasoned refutation by Sushil Kumar Saxena[9]. In a famous passage, Bradley himself states clearly his position:

I will state the case briefly thus. Find any piece of existence, take up anything that anyone could possibly call a fact, or could in any sense assert to have being, and then judge if it does not consist in sentient experience. Try to discover any sense in which you can still continue to speak of it, when all perception and feeling have been removed; or point out any fragment of its matter, any aspect of its being, which is not derived from, and is not still relative to this source. When the experiment is made strictly [controlled by theoretical reason], I can think of nothing else than the experienced. Anything, in no sense felt or perceived becomes to me quite unmeaning. As I cannot try to think of it without realizing either that I am not thinking at all, or that I am thinking of it against my will as being experienced[10].

In opposition to Wollheim, I judge that Bradley has successfully argued his case. I have attempted the experiment suggested, which has led me to conclude with Bradley. To the degree that the imagination is employed by Bradley, it is under the control of "thought", viz., theoretical reasoning. Wollheim's type of critique misconstrues Bradley radically. If Wollheim had formulated correctly Bradley's premise, his construction could have functioned as an outline of Bradley's argumentation and served as a model for critical discussion. But he did not do so. With the correction of "combined" to "being indissolubly one with" experience, Wollheim's modelling of Bradley's thought could have offered a valid point for discussion—one, I have noted, Bradley won. Whatever, Bradley used a different terminology from Reininger, but proposed the same kind of analysis as that expound by Reininger. So, let us now turn to Reininger.

Though Reininger, like Bradley, makes use of his very own speculating consciousness as the object of investigation (not possessing anyone else's) such that he does not intend to limit his thesis to human consciousness, viz., to the mere *mind*, a restriction that constitutes the source of Rescher's understanding of idealism. If Bradley is correct, Rescher is wrong in his limitation of conscious activity merely to the mind. Insofar as Rescher embraces idealism, it is a *conceptual* idealism, an idealism that is compatible with his realism, which means that independence remains the prime feature reality. Independence obligates consciousness to agree with the object, which results in affirming truth as *adequatio ad rem*, viz., as correspondence to the autonomy of reality from consciouseness.

Reininger, of course, rejects such autonomous separating off of reality from consciousness as expressed in his theorem of consciousness. Reininger makes his case explicating this theorem:

(It) follows immediately from [the theorem] that no statements about an absolutely non-conscious thing/entity [*ein schlechthin Unbewußtes*] could be possible, even in the form of a recognition that it [= a thing totally be-yond consciousness, viz., *das schlechthin Un-bewußt-es*] "is". ... The theo-rem of consciousness [*Bewußtsein*] does not in itself exclude in any way that there can be a being outside of consciousness [of a mind, i.e., a finite consciousness] and that it can be thought according to its own concept, which in that case it would have ceased to be a thing absolutely not per-taining to consciousness [*ein schlechthin Nicht-Bewußtes*]. Let *one attempt to* direct *one's thinking toward an absolutely non-conscious thing [or a thing absolutely independent of consciousness, i.e., ein schlechthin Un-bewußtes]*! Not only can I know nothing about something in any way not pertaining to consciousness [*von einem in keiner Weise Bewußten*], but I cannot even say that I know nothing about it. Pertaining to consciousness [= *Bewußtheit*] is not a predicate which applies to somethings which one has to do and not to others. It [*Bewußtheit*] is rather a characteristic which cannot be thought away [in total contradiction of Wollheim, to all realism], it is the <u>character</u> <u>indelibilis</u> of everything that can become the object of our reflection (*MW*, 23-24). (Italics added)

Reininger's formulation is more complex and more profound than that of Brad-ley's, although, alas, an English translation can neither express adequately nor fully that meaning without radically rewriting Reininger's words. Of importance is that both Bradley and Reininger express in principle the same thesis; namely, it is not possible to conceive in any meaningful way an object supposedly totally ab-sence of being cognized *per se,* of being enveloped by consciousness. Bradley makes a rationally controlled thought experiment which, despite all efforts, can-not find any meaning, any semantic content whatsoever relative to an object sup-posedly free of all "being-for-consciousness". I suggest doing the same with Rein-inger's suggestion. Philosophical discussion only encounters something meaning-ful according to Bradley in terms of "being present in experience". I suggest to the reader that he/she duplicate Bradley's search for what has no necessary connec-tion with "experience" or take up Reininger's search for that which does not per-tain to consciousness. If the reader finds meaning, I ask that he/she bring this dis-covery to (my) consciousness, which is in this matter as cognitively frustrated as Bradley's. Reininger for his part achieves, I contend, a superior conceptualization. This contention is persuasive, i.e., in no way whatsoever can anyone say anything whatsoever about *"ein schlechthin Unbewußtes"*, viz., about a supposed object characterized by not "pertaining to consciousness" (*"Bewußtheit"*) in any way whatsoever. Following Reininger, I contend that the object itself must not only be intrinsically cognizable in order *to be (Sein, esse)*, but also—and of necessity—it must entail *being cognized* in order *to be (Sein, esse)* at all—such is the *character indelibilis* that lies at the central ontological claim of idealism. In other words, it grounds the "ontology of idealism". Most realists will grant that the object, when not cognized, is potentially cognizable, while contemporaneously *rejecting* that an object *qua* real has being (*esse, Sein*) only as "being-cognized", viz., "being-present" to consciousness *per se*. Realists consider the cognitional state to be a mere accidental relation. It is for this reason that the object as *cognizable* according to realism possesses the *character indelibilis* of **independence** from *being cognized*—so the "ontology of realisms", however much they otherwise disagree with one another. For ontological idealism, on the other hand, the indissolubleness of *is-cognizing* and *being-cognized* constitute the *character indelibilis* of mutual **dependency** between being (*Sein*) and consciousness (*Bewußtsein*). *Pertaining to consciousness* constitutes and establishes the extensional coincidence of the being of reality (*Wirkichkeit*) as a non-relational oneness. The indissoluble oneness cannot be thought away, and it is not a predicate to be applied to some beingS or things and not others, rather it is *the* feature of the non-relational oneness of experience and the experienced as experience (Bradley), viz., consciousness (Reininger).

In order that no confusion occurs relative to the primacy of consciousness, I stress that said consciousness is, as Reininger contends, extensionally one with *being* (*esse, Sein*, être, *to be*). The English term "being" is very poor, misleading, misdirecting, hence confusing for ontological thinking. This is so because it ambiguously compounds "to be"/*esse* and "(a) being"/*ens*. It should be relentlessly eliminated from philosophy in English, which is naught but a pipe dream. Consequently, I must use said philosophical term as the use of "to be" can sound weird in certain contexts. *Being* (*Sein*) and *consciousness* (*Bewußtsein*) share the one and the same indissoluble extensionality. What *is*, is *present to* consciousness!!! But in whose "consciousness"??? The consciousness here intended is **not** the consciousness of the human "mind", viz., of any finite awareness; the "mind" being so often used to characterize idealism, particularly by realists (e.g., Rescher). If consciousness is limited to the human mind, then realism is correct, though it leads one into an epistemological *cul-de-sac*. Unfortunately for realists, they have not been able (I believe) to depict, describe, theorize or make semantical comprehensible the non-nonsensical nature of "independence" from cognition.

If the reader has accepted the challenge and failed to refute Bradley or Reininger, the reader is, *nolens, volens*, an idealist, at least latently, however unconformable idealism might make such a "discovery" of one's identity nowadays. If the reader has found a refutation of the idealist pair discussed, then said reader, now a convinced realist, will have little interest in following the ensuing argumentation. This argumentation, particularly relative to Royce's reflections, assumes an idealist ontology.

Royce's idealism as the prerequisite to his "ontological argument": We can now turn briefly to Royce's idealist reflections. His proof of the Absolute of idealism in the form of an "ontological argument" obtains it probative force only in the context of idealism as outlined in the previous section. Simply put: reality (= shared extension of being and consciousness) as understood by idealism is the presupposition for an ontological argument. Let us recall Wolfgang Röd' pithy definition of the ontological argument.

> The ontological argument ... [consists in] ... the intent to prove the existence of God solely on the basis of definitions and nominally on the basis of the definition of 'God' in accord with certain ontological axioms ... [11].

The key point is that the "certain ontological axioms" must be well understood before an adequate evaluation of the ontological argument is possible. In short, there is no point in attempting to prove or disprove any given version of the argument without first examining, judging and critiquing the axioms that lend to the argument its rationality and that constitute the framework from which the proof can be meaningfully argued for or against. If a critic ignores this background, he will have effectively treated the axioms as irrelevant or unworthy of reflection and, most likely, will show himself to be lacking in his understanding of the ontological proof concerned. James A. Lindsay thrusts St. Anselm's ontological proof into the historical trash bin of worthless thinking concluding:

> [Anselm's] argument for the existence of God, a stupendous game of wordplay, centered upon a definition of God as "that than which nothing higher can be conceived[12].

Despite Lindsay's otherwise frivolous deconstruction of Anselm, it is to his credit that he does note that there was some type of Neoplatonism floating about during Anselm's time (and, I add, in me), implying an influence upon Anselm. More important is some reference to infinity. An inquisitive insight, however, is lacking. Anselm in his *Proslogion* (1077/78 AD) did claim that God is "aliquid quo nihil maius cogitari possit" / "something about which nothing greater can be thought"[13]. Anslem 's interpreters and critics often focus upon this contention for their evaluation of his argument, overlooking other concepts that Anselm introduced. Anselm's notion is not specifically mathematical, yet it does seem to refer to infinity. Although Anselm did not use the Latin *"infinitum"*, he did use *"incircumspectum"* many times, a term meaning the same as infinity, only expressed metaphorically in a different manner. In the theoretical background to the notion of infinity lurks the paradoxical contrast of "unbounded", the "all-encompassing" and the "whole"—ideas of supreme interest to Royce. In the framework of his idealism, Royce effectively selects for his starting point Anselm's "something greater than which nothing can be thought", namely God! Why? Within the axioms of idealism, consciousness and being are one and constitute all there is, i.e.,

Reality. There is nothing that is not present to consciousness *per se* as the necessary correlative to all that is *per se*. For this reason, Royce establishes a conception of God adequate to idealism's version of consciousness[14]. He insists that

> the reality that we seek to know has always to be defined as that which either is or would be present to a sort of experience which we ideally define as an organized ... experience. We have, in point of fact, no conception of reality capable of definition except this one (*CG*, 168).

Royce presents his view of reality (admittedly influenced by Bradley) by negating the idea of anything beyond consciousness, in other words, any supposed

> beyond [experience] is itself content of an actual experience, the experience to which the beyond is presented being in such intimate relation to the experience which asserts the possibility, that both must be viewed as aspects of the one whole, fragments of the one organization.

We have here a repetition of the fundamental theses of Bradley and of Reininger and, at the same time, *in nuce* the heart of his argument, namely: What is, is *not* beyond experience, rather it is being *for* consciousness. Being and consciousness are *indissolubly* one—this is the idealistic ontology just explained. Royce's embracing of the idealistic paradigm is evident and constitutes the prerequisite for the cogency of his argumentation. If a reader rejects the theoretical reasoning of Reininger and Bradley, then Royce's proof too will fail its appointed task. But what advantage did Royce achieve by prefacing his ontological argument delineating idealism's unity of consciousness with being "God", rather than say as the Absolute? The Absolute of traditional Anglo-Saxon idealism (e.g., Bradley, Taylor, Bosanquet, Sprigge, etc.) can appear to be obtusely abstract in explanation, basically comprehensible only to the adepts. So, Royce sought to avail himself of a recognizable, traditional definition, one having more content for his readers, yet clearly entailing reference to an absolute consciousness enveloping all being. Royce clearly fulfils Röd's definition of the ontological argument writing:

> I propose to define, in advance, what we mean under the name "God," by means of using what tradition would call one of the Divine Attributes. I refer here to what has been called the attribute of Omniscience, or of the Divine Wisdom. By the word "God" I shall mean, a being who is conceived as possessing in the full all logically possible knowledge [= full awareness of all things in all aspects that are], insight, wisdom. Our problem, then, becomes at once this: does there demonstrably exist an Omniscient being? Or is the concept of an Omniscient Being, for all that we can say, a bare ideal of the human mind. (*CP*, 7).

Royce's strategy was clearly aimed at not only the die-hearted idealist, but also at those whose thinking does not abode in the kingdom of idealism. By modeling his definition of "God" on St. Thomas Aquinas, well known to the all, be they idealists and realists alike, Royce was able to direct his reflections to a broader field of readers.

> But the conception of the Divine that St. Thomas reached remains in certain important aspects identical [to Royce's notion of an Absolute] I think with the definition that I have tried to repeat. … I am certainly disposed to insist that what the faith of our fathers has genuinely meant by God is, despite all the blindness and unessential accidents of religious tradition, identical with the inevitable outcome of reflective philosophy [of idealism] CG, 40-50)

Royce has in effect translated the Absolute (Consciousness) of Idealism into terms that, among others, the realist followers of Thomas Aquinas would find comprehensible. The term is notoriously vague at times, so it behooves me to give it some meaning. The Absolute *per se* entails, as J. N. Findlay has shown, the notion of ultimacy[15]. Findlay comments:

> An Absolute is, first of all, an entity, an existent, something that is, in the fullest and highest sense permitted by ontology … . But, whatever our ontology, an Absolute, if admitted, must be placed in the supreme category of that ontology, and not in any reducible or dependent segment (*AA*, 21-22). …

> … The position of an Absolute, as an existent which cannot *not* exist, certainly has some odd features: if it may exist, it certainly does exist and exists of necessity, which suggests that we can infer its existence from its mere possibility. … That the possibility of its existence coincides with its necessary existence, means, in fact, that its existence is only possible if its existence represents the only possibility … (*AA*, 23). …

> We are, in short, *in quest* of an Absolute having the highest conceivable degree of mutual requiredness among it essential members or features, so that the thought of each, trained only on each, inevitably pushes us to the thought of all the others. … But we should wish to move as far in the direction of the Anglo-Saxon idealists as our ideal material allows, and we should never gratuitously suppose *independence* and relative contingency among the more rooted or pervasive features of the world (*AA*, 25). (Italics added.)

Although Royce articulates the highest degree of Reality in the terms of Christian theology, he certainly understands the Christian "God" as essentially compatible with the Absolute of idealism. The Absolute Consciousness of Royce's idealism evinces omniscience as much as does Aquinas' conception of God.

> You can ... define the Absolute as Thought. But then you mean ... a thought that sees its own fulfilment in the world of its self-possessed life ... . Such an Absolute Thought you can also call, in its wholeness a Self; for it beholds [= consciousness acting] the fulfilment [= present to consciousness], and views the determined character of its living experience [consciousness] with what its universal conceptions mean. All these names: "Absolute Self," "Absolute Thought," "Absolute Experience," are ... equally valuable expressions of different aspects of the same truth. God is known as Thought [consciousness] fulfilled; as absolutely organised, so as to have one ideal unity of meaning; as Truth, transparent to itself; as Life in absolute accordance with idea; as selfhood eternally obtained (*CG*, 45-46).

Royce considered his conception of the Absolute to be basically the same "conception of the Divine that St. Thomas reached [and] remains in certain important respect central, in essence, I think, with the definition I have tried to repeat", (*CG*, 49). I do not see that Royce in any meaningful way has falsified either the position of the Absolute of Anglo-Saxon idealism or the "God" of Christianity as conceived by Thomas Aquinas relative to the attribute of omniscience. By using God defined as omniscient, Royce thereby specifies in Christian terms the function of consciousness in its indissoluble oneness with being (*Sein*, *esse*, *to be*) of the idealist conception. Royce clearly states

> that an Omniscient Being would possess an Absolute Experience; that is, a whole complete or self-contained experience, not a mere part of some larger whole (CG, 13-14).

Infinite consciousness is the defining attribute of Being, i.e., it is being *qua* omnisciently consciousness—leaving Royce in the idealist tradition from Bradley through Reininger, though not in opposition to the realism of Thomas Aquinas. For the sake of argument, Royce problematizes this indissoluble oneness by suggesting, however, that perhaps the notion of God he has developed is no more than mere theoretical "possibility", certainly no proven "actuality", just a problematic thought selected by Royce in order to show rationally that mere possibility is not, paradoxically, possible[16]. This "showing" is the ontological argument. It should not be surprising, based on my above analysis of idealist ontology, that Royce supports his ontological argument illustrating the realm of idealism outlined above. What, one might well ask, is a "possibility"?

Royce' ontological argument: I remind the reader as I do myself that for idealism there is no meaning whatsoever to being (*esse*), beings (*ens/entia*), reality (*Wirklichkeit*; *Realität*) "beyond", viz., *independent of* experience *per se*, "beyond", viz., *independent of* consciousness *per se*, **period**! The *indissoluble* oneness between being (*esse/ens-entia*) and experience (consciousness) does not reside in the human *mind*, nor in the minds of all humans, for they are, each and every one, fragmentary (= limited to an individual field of consciousness—> Chapter 2). The affirmation of *omniscient* "Absolute Experience (= comparatively the *omniscient* God of Christianity), that is, a whole complete or self-contained experience" derives from the necessity of a common world, a common reality, relative to which humans with their minds are but limited self-reflecting fragments. Consequently, the idealist paradigm is the result of a critical, theoretical, rational investigation of experience *per se* and without which there is no world to talk about. The claim, say, that said conceptualization of God is but a possibility remaining "beyond" any analysis of what is self-evidently experienced, only provable by some sort of causal argument is a puzzle for idealism. The conceptualization itself *qua* possibility is not doubted. In other words, the interpretation of reality as absolute experience (Bradley) or omniscience (Aquinas) is a valid conceptualization of the Absolute or of God, i.e., it entails no contradiction, a least on a *prima facie* level. Royce and Aquinas, both hold that such "omniscience" embodies not just an idea, but rather definitely refers to reality. For a Thomas Aquinas God is certainly real, a necessary existing "is". However, Aquinas does not think that human reason (partial agreement with Kant) can conclude rationally to the reality of an omniscient God simply by means of examining his conceptualization of God, which is of course the thesis of the ontological argument. For Aquinas, if God is real, then the highest Reality, God, is in fact omniscient. No question about that. However, knowing that an omniscient God is, enables *no* rational conclusion at all that God exists. The Jesuit historian of philosophy, F. C. Copleston, quotes Aquinas contending in his *Summa Theologica*: "No one can think the opposite of that which is self-evident. ... But the opposite of the proposition 'God exists' can be thought. ... Therefore the proposition that God exists is not self-evident"[17]. Copleston explains Aquinas:

> This refusal to allow that God's existence is a self-evident truth for the human mind is closely bound up with what I have called the 'empiricist side of Aquinas' philosophy [and I would add 'realist side']. Our knowledge begins with sense-experience, and on account of man's psychological constitution material things constitute the primary natural object of the human mind. Any natural knowledge which we have of a being [God] or beings [angels] transcending the visible [= empirical] world is obtained by reflection [reasoning] on the data of experience (*A*, 113).

Because it is supposedly possible to conceive the world as void of omniscient consciousness, Thomism permits a conceptualization of the world in materialist and/or naturalist terms—only to be denied because Thomas has proved that there is a non-visible reality called God. The gapping difference, the incommensurate opposition, between the realist philosophy of Aquinas and that of idealists (German idealism, Anglo-American idealism and Austrian idealism) is evident. I take this to be quite "self-evident". Idealists, in contrast to realists, consider "experience" or "consciousness" to be an analytically ascertainable feature, a *character indelibilis*, of being, existence, reality and, as such, should be a constitutive part of any metaphysics. Consciousness does not characterize realism as a necessary, viz., indissoluble feature, even if the realist does himself believed to have demonstrated realities, being(s) in the transcendent realm, whereas idealism in contrast does. The mutually exclusiveness between the transcendent non-visible realm and the immanent visible realm of empirical material world is a function of the "independence" typical of realism. (I will make a final word on my position relative to immanence and transcendence, already anticipated in Chapter 3, at the end of this epilogue, it probably will be seen as a compromise between idealism and realism.) The mutual aversion between idealism and realism as defined in this epilogue was a motivational factor for Royce's pursuit of the idealist paradigm. Before diving into the problematic between Aquinas and Royce regarding the "self-evidence" for the ontological argument, I find it advisable to turn to Royce's "summary of the whole argument for the reality of the omniscient" (*CG*, 42f). (In this context I once again refer to Chapter 2 of this book.) Royce summarizes thus:

> Let us sum up, in a few words, our whole argument. There is, for us as we are, experience [consciousness]. Our thought [rational analysis] undertakes the interpretation of this experience. Every intelligent interpretation of an experience involves however, the appeal from experienced fragment [the individual field of consciousness] some more organized whole of experience, in whose unity this fragment is conceived as finding its organic place [= the common world in which all partial, yet individual experiences participate which in turn is experience]. To talk of any reality which this fragmentary experience indicates is to conceive reality as the content of the more organized experience. To assert that there is any absolutely real fact indicated by our experience, is to regard this reality as presented to an absolutely organized experience, in which every [experiencing] fragment finds its place (*CG*, 42).

The realism of Aquinas & Co finds in empirical experience *qua* experiencing *per se* no grounds for integrating such consciousness as a fundamental clue to what reality is or even if there is an all-encompassing reality—which must be proved to be or to exist. Consciousness, the bane of materialism, seems to be equally an irrelevancy or of secondary importance for Thomist realism relative to the construction of metaphysical theory. More on this theme below.

Let us turn to Royce's discussion of an omniscient God is non-contradictory (and I assume here no objection) is *in truth* only a possibility. What does a possibility entail? Royce informs us:

> But, now, there can be no such thing as a merely possible *truth* apart from some actual experience. To say: So and so is possible, is to say: There is, somewhere in experience, an actuality some aspect of which can be defined in terms of this possibility. A possibility is a truth expressed in terms of a proposition bringing with *if*, or a hypothetical proposition,—and *is* expressed in the terms of an *if*. For you cannot define a truth as concretely true unless you define it as really present to some experience. Thus ... I cannot believe in the truth of such a supposition [that I make] without believing in some concrete and experienced fact (*CG*, 36-37). (At his point, I do suggest that my reader turn to Chapter 2 on the "being of truth".)

Royce's response is fully in accord with the ontology of his idealism.

> So far, indeed, in speaking of reality and an absolute experience, one talks of mere conceptual objects,—one deals, as the mathematical science does, with what appear to be only shadowy Platonic ideas. Do these Platonic ideas of the absolute reality, and of the absolutely organized experience, stand for anything but merely ideal or possible entities? The right answer to this question comes, if one first assumes, for argument's sake, that the answer is negative, and that there is no organized, but only a fragmentary experience (*CG*, 42).

In Chapter 2 this problem was dealt within the terms of the limitations of my solipsistic assumed "my field of consciousness", which I found not to be theoretically sustainable because such a phenomenological solipsism could not handle the problem of error—error indicating reality beyond my conscious field, my fragmentary experience. Phenomenology had to give way to ontology. If an all-encompassing experience/consciousness is just a mere possibility and not ascertainable by analysis, what then is to ask:

> But hereupon arises the question: What reality has this fact of the limitation and fragmentariness of the actual world of experiences? If every reality has to exist just in so far as there is experience of its existence [= prime ontological principle of idealism], then the determination of the world of experience to be this world and no other, the fact that reality contains no other facts than these, is, as the supposed in all reality, itself the object of one experience, for which the fragmentariness of the finite world appears as a presented and absolute fact, beyond which no reality is to be viewed as even genuinely possible. ... But ... this final experience is the hypothesis

forthwith defined as One, as all-inclusive, as determined by nothing beyond itself, as assured of the complete fulfilment of its own ideas concerning what is,—in brief, it becomes an absolute experience. The very effort to deny an absolute experience involves, then, the actual assertion of such an absolute experience (*CG*, 43).

But, certainly it is possible to formulate a thesis that the world lacks any central unity or that REALITY is beyond experience? At least by hypothesis?? A hypothesis is, well, nothing but speculation, a suggestion of the way things perhaps are. That is not the problem. Is the suggestion, however, true or not? Indeed, what is the being of a question and its answer? Royce immediately interrupts:

> The very watch word, then, of our whole doctrine is this: All knowledge is of something experienced. For this means that nothing actually exists save what is somewhere experienced … [and what] constitutes the very essence of the world of finite experience, is, as positive reality, somewhere so experienced in its wholeness that this entire constitution of the finite appears as a world beyond which, in its whole constitution, nothing exists or can exist. But, for such an experience … every finite incompleteness … appears as a part of a whole in whose wholeness the fragments find their true place, the ideas their realization, the seeking its fulfilment, and our whole life its truth so its eternal rest … (*CG*, 46-47).

Let the reader not forget the premise of idealism, namely that

> one must be serious with this concept of experience. Reality, as opposed to illusion, means simply an actual or possible content of experience, not in so far as this experience is supposed to be transient and fleeting, but in so far as it is conceived to be somehow inclusive and organized, the fulfilment of a system of ideas, the answer to a scheme of rational questions (*CG*, 32).

A mere hypothesis is possible, no doubt there. But the realization of the "pure desire to know" truth about reality as it is allows for no mere, bare possibility regarding truth. Truth too has its being (cf. Chapter 2).

> Now, to regard our experience as suggesting truth is, as we have seen, to mean that our experience indicates what a higher or inclusive, *i.e.* a more organized, experience world find presented thus or thus to itself. (*CG*, 39)

> In fine, if there is an actual experience to which an absolute reality corresponds, then you can indeed translate this actuality into the terms of bare possibility. But unless there is actual experience, the bare possibility expresses no truth (*CG*, 38).

With the words of Royce just cited, I conclude my exposition of Royce's ontological proof as a function of idealist ontology. Also I recommend again turning to Chapter 2 of this book for more on truth. I trust that the "axioms" (Röd) underlying and grounding said ontological proof have been presented, explained such that my reader understands their contribution to the argument. As I remember, Johan Gottlieb Fichte (1762-1814), the first of the great German idealists, once suggested that there are "convincing" arguments both for realism and idealism, leaving it to the interested thinker to choose for himself—and, furthermore, said choice would probably be a function of the character a person has. I can accept Fichte's thesis, only I understand by "character" as the zeitgeist of the times. At one period in the cultural history or Germany or of England and America, the character of the times would have easily absorbed and, with pleasure, intellectually digested the idealism expounded above and throughout this study. But those days have slipped away, a hard realism reigns, the fertile plains of idealism have given away, ravaged dry by the arid winds of realism, particularly of a reductive type leading to materialism. Idealism has fallen so much out of style in the Western world of the 21st Century, that my semi-humorous invitation at the end of Chapter 4 still stands. That isle, that Elysium of idealist joy, still abounds with open condominiums awaiting the arrival of those who live the days of long ago. Reservations?

Final Word (or not too many more): Chapter 3 dealt with the problem of infinity. I sought to understand the concept of infinity by paying attention to the method used to derive it. To my surprise, two concepts were discovered because there are two ways of constructing a notion of infinity. One way—the normal way throughout history—has been to extrapolate. Hence, the recital of the natural numbers is: 1, 2, 3, ...∞ constitutes an extrapolation. This method has led to innumerable difficulties, which for a while were apparently solved by Georg Cantor with his many infinities and his set theory as the basis for arithmetic. Michael Huemer, in a book very welcomed to me with my penchant for Socratic irony, writes:

> Conclusion: Set theory is not the foundation of arithmetic, let alone of all mathematics. The rejection of sets therefore would not undermine the foundations of mathematics in any interesting sense. ...
>
> ... Strictly speaking, there are no infinite quantities: There is no cardinal number greater than all the natural numbers, nor is there any number larger than all the real numbers[18].

In just two short sentences, Cantor orthodoxy meats its heterodox arch heretic, and falls. The theoretical difficulties entailed in the infinity of the *extrapolatory* method are enormous and have elicited much theoretical debate. The so-derived concept intimates, however, another possibility, indeed, another method which is the *exclusionary* derivation of infinity. As the adjective suggests, all finitude is excluded from this second—and apparently brand new—interpretation of infinity. In Chapter 3, I tried to draw out some rather startling conclusions from an examination of exclusionary infinity. The reader is referred to the chapter. The reader might ask why I am reprinting this publication on infinity. What does it have to do with the summation now being written. In very brief terms, I shall try to answer the query.

Royce, if not most British idealists, specifically Bradley and Bosanquet, have been accused of pantheism, though I think panentheism would be a more accurate designation. Royce reacted very negatively to the charge of pantheism; indeed, he appended, as was often his custom, a *long* essay to the book: "The Absolute and the Individual: Supplementary Essay by Professor Royce (*CG*, 135-348) in which the individual was closely examined and not absorbed by the Absolute as is want in pantheism. I think Royce argued with success relative to pantheism, particularly if I compare him to a self-confessing pantheist. The Iranian Reza Aslan has expressed *in nuce* the relation between God and man that typifies his pantheism. He writes, and I translate:

> Perhaps we ought to consider the possibility of the fact that the motive for why we have the cognitive impulse to think of God as a divine reflection of our own proper I is because *all and each one of us*, we are God[19].

Correlative to each and every one of us being God is the logical conclusion that God is each and every one of us. That is pantheism in a concrete form. In no way can one reduce Royce to that sort of a pantheism[20]. Certain it is that Royce never considered the individual to be God nor viewed God to be all individuals. Perhaps, one could interpret Hegel in this direction. Perhaps not. Royce for his part was interested in the *salvation* of the individual, not conceived as God, but as related to God[21]. If Reza is a typical illustration of pantheism, then Royce was surely not a pantheist. The pantheist needs no salvation, just rational insight into his ontological status as God and God as al individuals, then all will be right. Whereas Royce is free from the accusation of being a pantheist, he is not free from the accusation that he—like many idealists—was a pan*ent*heist, i.e., that God and the world constitute some sort of continuity, a monad, though God (infinitude) and man (finitude) are different, God transcending in some way the manifold of beings, but not evidencing any full ontological separation or total "otherness". Relative to the panentheistic model, I contend, a similar structural relationship pertains between the extrapolatory notion of infinity and the infinity of natural numbers. Infinity, ∞, is not the greatest natural number completing, finishing off the infinite series of numbers, it is a statement of endlessness. Nevertheless, within the series itself, constituting the augmentation order of the numbers, each higher number seemingly approaches ever closer to infinity, but—and here is the rub—the series is always less an end, is endless, which means that each and every number in its numerical value remains *endlessly* distant from infinity. No natural number approaches infinity more than any other one. The prime feature of *extrapolatory* infinity must be conceived as "endlessness"—a magnitude value that never changes. The feature of "endlessness" is not a final value beyond the endlessly augmenting natural numbers, falsely suggested by the use of the linear symbolism "... ∞" in order to lend a finish to the series. Instead, it is the form, the ordering immanent to the very *seriality* of natural numbers in the series; hence ∞ is both immanent to each and every number, yet transcends each and *all* numbers. Interestingly, we are left effectively with a mathematical pan*EN*theism. All this is absent from exclusionary infinity.

From the point of view of *exclusionary* infinity, it is clear, the ascription "endlessness" to *actual* infinity makes no sense, since having an "end" only has meaning within the terms of finitude, which has been *excluded* from infinity. As a pure magnitude, exclusionary infinity radically *transcends* all finite numbers, both individually and collectively, it is not the form of their seriality, it is their unattainable value *par excellence*. Because I have as yet no name for said infinity of exclusion, I've borrowed from Cantor a designation he used for God, namely *absolutum*. The adjective "ab-solute" means etymologically "to be cut off" or "sliced away from". The *absolutum* is fundamentally distinct (not just different), viz., cut off from finitude whatever the finite enormity might be. Each and every, all numbers, do not really approach infinity as mathematicians are wont to say. Why? Each numerical value is *endlessly* distant from infinity. For instance, 100,000 is not any closer to infinity than 1, both fall *endlessly* short of the infinite, though 100,000 is further distant from 0 than 1—and that is the distance that imparts enormity. From an exclusionary point of view, endlessness is equated with the *absolutum*. Exclusionary infinity is cut off, separated and distinct from all finite realities, i.e., I is absolute. Exclusionary infinity is simply *radically other than* finitude. By being-cut-off-from finitude, exclusionary infinity possesses no negativity, hence it can be viewed as pure positivity. Relative to the notion of *absolutum* as actual infinity, I find myself necessitated to place Royce (also Bradley and Anglo-American idealists) into the camp of panENtheists. What this means for my idealism versus the idealism of Royce and other absolute idealists will be touched on below. First I want to pointedly indicate why I view Royce was panentheistic, probably most Anglo-American idealists too.

The same procedure used to conceive reality as infinite is entailed in conceiving infinite reality as eternal. Infinity and eternity have their respective etymologies, one from space and the other from time. Eternity is not everlasting time, it is not time going on and on *ad infinitum*, ever progressing temporally thither, so on and so on, etc., etc. etc. That is a feature of time and not of eternity. Time per definition entails an ongoing and hence a changing sequence—and it is precisely "sequential changeableness" that seems to be at variance with eternity. I experience this difficulty, perhaps, antinomy, when Royce writes:

> *Temporal.* Is the world order, because, so far as we can know, time is the universal form of the expression of the Will. *Eternal* is the same world order, because past, present, and future time equally belong to the Real, and their Being implies, by definition, that they are present, in their wholeness, to the final insight. And Time, surveyed in its wholeness, is Eternity[22].

If time entails change, motion, difference, the new (novelty), then the idea that time could possess "wholeness" is difficult to understand. The natural numbers of an infinite series do not and cannot obtain "wholeness", having no intrinsic end! Any finite value of any number is "endlessly" distant from infinity. This "endlessness" also applies to time. Any point t_1 in a series of infinitely progressing times is no closer to wholeness than $t_{100,000}$, so on and so on *ad infinitum*. The "wholeness" of exclusionary infinity is peculiar to it, i.e., it does not contain any finitude, rather the wholeness consists in the absence, in the 0 presence, of any finite number. Only the *absolutum* is whole, not a series without an end. I do not see how time can be equated with eternity because time cannot be "surveyed in its wholeness", no more than the series of natural numbers can be "surveyed in its wholeness". Thomas Schärtl has outlined his (and the eternalist's) understanding of eternity:

1   An eternal being is not just an everlasting entity. It is, literally, not subject to the flow of time.

Therefore:

2   A eternal being has no temporal parts. And:

3   An eternal being is 'simultaneous' to any points t_1 and t_2 in time even if t_1 and t_2 are not simultaneous.

4   An eternal being is, based on this notion of simultaneity, fully present (omnipresent to and at every point of time[23].

The vision of Royce and that of Schärtl clash. Schärtl's understanding is compatible and commensurate with my understanding of an exclusionary infinity. Whereas Royce unites the world with the Absolute/God, Schärtl separates the two realities. My interest here is not to argue for Schärtl against Royce. I only wish to justify reprinting Chapter 3 with its two conceptualizations of infinity. I have not entered into matter deeply, other than what writing a few words might produce. Should I attempt a serious consideration, I would not be writing this epilogue as a summation, rather as an extremely long chapter or even two chapters. Such an undertaking would alter the integrity of this book and turn it into an amalgamation of two books. For some intellectual fun, I will finish my book here suggesting—no more—a way in which creation could take place in the terms of infinity.

One of the great mathematicians was Srinivasa Ramanujan (1887-1920), a largely self-taught genius who literally dazzled the mathematicians of Cambridge, England in the early 20th Century. Robert Kangil in his biography of Ramanujan writes:

> Later in England, Ramanujan would build a theory of reality around zero and infinity, though his friend never quite figured out what he was getting at. Zero, it seemed, represented Absolute Reality. Infinity, or ∞, was the myriad manifestations of that Reality Their mathematical product, $\infty \times 0$, was not one number [countable something], but all the numbers [applied to the countable things] each of which corresponded to the individual acts of creation[24].

Let me transform Ramanujan's formula somewhat into the terms of exclusionary infinity. Exclusionary infinity contains 0 finite numbers, this is its actuality of fullness. Yet, although exclusionary infinity, the *absolutum*, possesses 0 actual expressions of finitude, that 0 is, nevertheless, not emptiness, not pure absence, rather *pure* fullness, *pure* positivity, in short, relative to finitude, pure potentiality. The act of creation is the actualization of this potentiality. It entails the insertion of negation into pure positivity. In this context, Ramanujan's ∞ refers to endless/infinite natural numbers; full diversity being the product of the zero-ness of absolute fullness being multiplied by endlessly diversifying negation. Such a multiplication produces the endless natural numbers or beings. Beautiful thought, but here offered as no more than as a possible consideration.

My reader, assuming acceptance or sympathy for my idealism, could well find it profitable to reflect upon the nature of infinity. Both the transcendent God of Thomas Aquinas or the imminent Reality in all finite manifoldness of Royce, both claim to be infinite. But, infinity is not infinity, i.e., there are two conceptions of infinity, extrapolative and exclusionary infinity. Whether Aquinas's view of the Absolute or Royce view of God is correct—that decision is left to my reader. With these words I do literally end this epilogue.

Footnotes

1   For Royce's "Relational Form of the Ontological Argument" see: *Royce, Metaphysics,* initially edited by William Ernest Hocking on Royce's Philosophy 9 Course of 1915-1916, (Albany: State University Press of New York, 1998), 115-142. For a discussion of the argument, and others, see William Ernest Hocking, "The Ontological Argument in Royce and Others" in *Contemporary Idealism in America,* (New York: The Macmillan Company, 1932), 43-66.

2   If one reads my critique of Sam Harris' argument against free will based on a materialism, it is easy to understand why I agree with Bernardo Kastrup's *Why Materialism is Baloney,* (Winchester, UK, Washington, USA: iff Books, 2014.

3   Cf. Rescher, A System of Pragmatic Idealism. Volume 1. *Human Knowledge in Idealistic Perspective,* (Princeton: Princeton University Press, 1992), 270. Hereafter referred to in the text as *SP!* Plus page number.

4   Lewis, *Mind and the World Order. Outline of a Theory or Knowledge,* (New York: Dover Publications, Inc.) 1929), 193-94.

5   Cf. Rescher, *Conceptual Idealism.* (Oxford: Basil Blackwell, 1973), 2-3. Hereafter referred to in the text as *CI* plus page number.

6   For a lengthy and weighty discussion of the coherence theory of truth, see Bland Branshard, *The Nature of Thought,* (London: George Allen & Unwin LTD, 1948), 212-332.

7   Cf. For Reininger's Explanation of the theorem, see Reininger, *Metaphysik der Wirklichkeit;* expanded 2nd. Edition, (München/Basel: Ernst Reinhardt Verlag, 1970, originally 1931), 23-28. Hereafter cited in the text as *MW* plus page number.

8   Cf. Wollheim, *F. H. Bradley,* (Middlesex: Peguin Books, 1959), 201. Hereafter cited in the text as *FHB* plus page number.

9   Cf. Saxena, *Studies in the Metaphysics of Bradley,* (London and New York: Routledge, 2014, originally 1967), 223-25. Saxena has written an excellent book on Bradley and defended him well.

10 *Bradley, Appearance* and Reality. *A Metaphysical Essay,* (Oxford: Clarendon Press, 1st edition 1893, 17th 1978), 127-128.

11 Cf. Röd, *Der Gott der reinen Vernunft: Die Auseinandersetzung um den ontologischen Gottesbeweis von Anselm,* (München: Beck, 1992), 13.

12   Cf. Linday, *Dot Dot Dot. Infinity Plus God Equals Folly,* (np: Lightening Source International, 2013), 175-83.

13   Anselm, *Proslogion,* Capitulum II. Because there are so many editions of Anselm Proslogion, I have only identified where in the text the quotation is taken from.

14   Royce, *The Conception of God. A Philosophical Discussion Concerning the Nature of the Divine Idea as a Demonstrable Reality;* (New York: The Macmillan Company, 1897.

15   Cf. Findlay, *Ascent to the Absolute,* (London: George Allen & Unwin LTD and New York: Humanities Press, 1970). For the introduction to the notion of the Absolute, cf. pages 17-38. Hereafter cited in the text as AA plus page number. Hereafter cited in the text as CG plus page number.

16   There is, however, an irreconcilable conflict between idealism and Thomism (assuming that that –ism reflects St. Thomas' genuine thinking). A Thomist, such as a towering figure like Antonio Millán-Puelles, treats in his philosophical lexicon the themes of "Teología Natural" and the feature most proper to God, namely "Ser [To be, Being] Necesario por sí" without mentioning consciousness even once, though never denying it. The is no mention that God is conscious, though attributes necessitating consciousness are listed. See, Millán-Puelles, *Léxico Filosófico,* Madrid: RIALP, 2002 (originally 1984), 518-27 and 549-58. The failure to conceptualize consciousness and being *(esse, Sein, To Be)* as an indissoluble oneness typifies Thomist philosophy up to now and, hence also, I think, realism. Despite his emancipation from St. Thomas, an outstanding thinker such as the Jesuit Bernard Lonergan, just cannot recognize the indissolubility of Being and Consciousness. (I have availed myself of Lonergan's theory of insight in Chapter 1 of this study). In his discussion of the notion of Being *per se* Lonergan writes perceptively: "Being, then is the objective of the pure desire to know. ... By the desire to know is meant the dynamic orientation manifested in question for intelligence and for reflections. ... The desire to know, then, is simply the inquiring spirit of man". *Quotation from Insight. A Study of Human Understanding,* (New York, San Francisco, London: Harper & Row, Publishers, 1978, originally 1958), 348. Despite some excellent discussions on the unity of consciousness in its intellectual mode of seeking to know, Lonergan does not mention consciousness and its role in the desire to know, let alone include consciousness as a feature of the unrestricted realm of being. What is unlimited relative to knowledge, namely *knowing,* is not mentioned as a feature of Being. In other words, Being, as the unrestricted object of unrestricted knowing (effectively "unrestricted"

= infinite), is distinct from the consciousness that is knowing, leaving Being per se, which is God, as a reality apparently dissoluble from consciousness (which is the point of realism). So, in some manner, being is intelligible—hence it attracts the pure desire to know—yet it is not noted that it "really" entails self-consciousness. I adventure to say that all realisms must prove consciousness. Lonergan attempts his proof of divine existence with an interesting syllogism. "If the real is being—I mean, the intelligible—then God exists; but the real is intelligible, the real is being; therefore, God exists". See Lonergan, *Understanding and Being*, in *Collected Works of Bernard Lonergan*, ed. Elisabeth A. Morelli and Mark D. Morlli, (Toronto, London, The University of Toronto Press, 2013, originally 1980). Apparently, God in His unrestricted Being is (not necessarily conscious). Lonergan was only a tiny theoretical step away from the Absolute of Bradley, but his realism blocked the passage.

17 Cf. Copleston, *Aquinas*, (London: Penguin Books, 1991, originally 1955), 111. Focusing on sense experience, Aquinas examines what we evidently "see", namely things in motion. At his point, Aquinas, based upon apparently self-evident metaphysical principles, applies a causal argument intending to show that a first cause is necessary for motion and that cause is God (who, however, is not acknowledged as conscious being). The nature and justification of causality in Thomism is not given like an empirical datum, one of the qualia, something that one sees floating about, rather it is derived from metaphysical "axioms" discovered by "pure" reason itself doing in effect the same rational activity interpreting motion, as Reininger does with the "datum" of consciousness. For some reason, "consciousness" is not mentioned by name by the scholastics/Thomists even as they seek to determine "primary attributes" of God. For instance, R. Garrigou-Lagrange, a most note-worthy Thomist, identifies God's principal attributes as "bonté, vie, sagesse, liberté, sainteté, mais la conciliation intime de ces perfections divines reste pour nous bien obscure". Cf. Garrigou-Lagrange, *DIEU. Son existence et sa Nature*, (Paris: Gabriel Beauchesne, 1923), 501. All the attributes noted certainly imply consciousness. Certainly Garrigou-Lagrange does not mean that, when God exercises his acts of love, He is unconscious while doing so? But the theologian does not explicitly inform the reader that the act is explicitly conscious. Consciousness as an attribute of God, and hence of "l'Être", is not examined. Taboo? This is true for other Thomists I have read such as Coffey, Wulf, Mercier, Sheen, Maritain, Gilson and many others. Consciousness as such plays no real role in primary reflections of Thomists and is treated by name only when consciousness of human beings becomes a matter of discussion (e.g. Feser), particularly relative to a biological context. This is not surprising as Thomists seek their

philosophical departure from what the senses present them, but not from the consciousness that is aware of the presented. To do that would constitute a possible entry into idealism.

18   Huemer, *Approaching Infinity*, (UK, USA: Palgrave Macmillan, 2016), 118 and 249.

19   Cf. Reza, *Dios. Una historia humana*; translated from English God. *A Human History* (2017), (Madrid: Taurus, 2019), 199.

20   T. L. S. Sprigge, in a masterful study of "absolute idealism", including Royce, argues that said idealism is in reality "pantheistic idealism". Cf. Sprigge, The *God of Metaphysics. Being a Study of the metaphysics and Religious Doctrines of Spinoza, Hegel, Kiergegaard, T. H. Green, Bernard Bosanquet, Josiah Royce, A. N. Whitehead, Charles Hartshorne, and Concluding with a Defence of Pantheistic Idealism,* (Oxford: Oxford University Press, 2008, originally 2006, 473-533. If Reza becomes the model for pantheism, then Spriggs's pantheism certainly contains some panentheism in it. Space allows for no serious critique, I can only recommend the book.

21   Cf. Royce, *The Sources of Religious Insight*, (Illinois: The Bross Lectures, 1911). Royce explains "that he [man], as he is, is in great danger of losing this highest good, so that his greatest need is of escape from this danger—whoever, I say, thus views our life, holds that man needs salvation" (no pages given in reprint) There is no need for "salvation" in Reza's views, only the need to cease being deceived, i.e., considering individuals to be other than God.

22   Cf. Royce, *The World and the Individual. Second Series. Nature, Man, and the Moral Order.* (Gloucester, Mass.: Dover Publictions, 1976, originally 1901), 337

23   Schärtl, "Why We Need God's Eternity: Some Remarks to Support a Classic Notion", in *God, Eternity, and Time,* edited by Christian Tapp and Edmund Runggaldier. London and New York: Routledge, 2016, originally 2011), 47-62, quotation from page 47.

24   Cf. Kangil, *The Man Who Knew Infinity. A Life of the genius Ramanujan.* London: Abacus, 1992), 66. I note that a movie has been made of Rmanujan's life with the title of the book.

Bibliography

Blanshard, Brand. *The Nature of Thought*. London: George Allen & Unwin LTD, 1948

Bradley, F. H. *Appearance and Reality. A Metaphysical Essay*. Oxford: Claredon Press, 1st edition 1893

Copleston, Frederick. *Aquinas*. London Penguin books, 1991, originally 1955.

Finlay, J. N. *Ascent to the Absolute*. London: George Allen & Unwin LTD New York: Huamanities Press, 1970.

Hocking, *William* Ernest. "The Ontological Argument in Royce and Others" in *Contemporary Idealism in America, edited by Clifford Barrett.* New York: The Macmillan Company, 1932, pp. 115-142.

Huemer, Michael. *Approaching Infinity*. UK, USA: Palgrave Macmillan, 2016.

Kanggil, Robert. *The Man Who Knew Infinity. A Life of the Genius Ramanujan-* London: Abacus, 1992.

Kastrup, Bernardo. *Why Materialism Is Baloney*. Winchester, UK, Washington, USA: ifff Books, 2014

Lewis, C. I. *Mind and the World Order. Outline of a Theory of Knowledge.* New York: Dover Publications, Inc., 1929

Linday, James A. *Dot Dot Dot. Infinity Plus God Equals Folly.* Np.: Lightening Source International, 2013.

Lonergan, Bernard. *Understanding and Being* in *Collected Works of Bernard Lonergan*, edited by Elisabeth Morelli and Mark D. Morelli. Toronto, London: The University of Toronto Press, 2013, originally 1980.

Millán-Puelles, Antonio. *Léxico Filosófico*. Madrid: RIALP, 2002, originally 1984.

Reza, Aslan. *Dios*. Translated from English into Spanish. Madrid: Taurus, 2019.

Reininger, Robert. *Metaphysik der Wirklichkeit*, expanded 2nd Edition. München/Basel: Ernst Rheinhardt Verlag, 1970, originally 1931.

Rescher, Nicolas. *A System of Pragmatic Idealism. Volume 1. Human Knowledge in Idealistic Perspective.* Princeton: Princeton University Press, 1992.

_____ , *Conceptual Idealism*. Oxford: Basil Blackwell, 1973.

Röd, Wolfgang. *Der Gott der reinen Vernunft: Die Auseinandersetzung um den ontologischen Gottesbeweis von Anselm.* München: Beck, 1992.

Royce, Josiah, Joseph le Comte and G. H. *The Conception of God. A Philosophical Discussion Concerning the Nature of the Divine Idea as a Demonstrable Reality*. New York: The Macmillan Company, 1897.

Royce, Josiah. *Metaphysics*, initially edited by William Ernest Hocking, reprint of Royce's Philosophy 9 Course, (Albany: State University Press New York, 1998.

_____, *The World and the Individual. Second Series. Nature, Man, and the Moral Order*. Gloucester, Mass.: Dover Publications, 1976, originally 1901.

Saxena, Sushil Kumar. *Studies in the Metaphysics of Bradley*. London and New York: Routledge, 2014, originally 1967.

Schärtl, Thomas. "Why We Need God's Eternity: Some Remark to Support a Classic Notion", in *God, Eternity, and Time*, edited by Christian Tapp and Edmund Runggaldier. London and New York: Routledge, 2016, originally 2011, 47-62.

Sprigge, T. L. S. *The God of Metaphysics*. Oxford: Oxford University Press, 2008.

Wollheim, Richard. *F. H. Bradley*. Middlesex Penguin Books, 1959.